BADGERS

Michael Clark

BADGERS

•MICHAEL CLARK•

with illustrations by
the author

Whittet Books

This book is dedicated to all badgers, to the memory of Eileen Soper, artist and defender of badgers, who was a neighbour, and to 'Boss Badger' himself, Dr Ernest Neal, who took me into another world when I read his first book *The Badger* and has patiently encouraged me in this interest ever since.

Half-title illustration: You have waited and waited and nearly given up as twilight has given way to darkness. Then comes that magical time of uncertainty: is it a black-and-white face or a trick of the moonlight? An ancient Briton stirs.
Title-page illustration: A badger family begins to explore outside its sett entrances on an early summer's evening.

First published 1988
Reprinted 1990, 1992
This revised edition published 1994
Text and illustrations © 1988, 1994 by Michael Clark
Whittet Books Ltd, 18 Anley Road, London W14 OBY

Design by Richard Kelly

British Library Cataloguing in Publication Data
Clark, Michael, 1943 -
    Badgers.
    1. Badgers —— Great Britain
    2. Mammals —— Great Britain
    I. Title
    599.74'447   QL737.C25
ISBN 0–905483–65–0

Typeset by Systemset Composition, London NW2
Printed and bound by WBC, Bridgend, Mid Glam.

Contents

Badgers are noted for their good housekeeping and their general grooming.

Acknowledgments

My thanks to Annabel Whittet and Pat Morris for suggesting I should try to write this book.

Very generous help and guidance has been provided by Dr Ernest Neal, who has done more to ensure the survival of badgers than anyone. He has given much advice on this project, and I cannot recall a time in the past thirty years when he has not given freely of his time to help me in my work on badgers whenever asked to do so. It has been an honour to work with him from the first days of the Mammal Society Badger Survey, through the years on the Government's Consultative Panel for Badgers and when I did the illustrations for his second monograph *Badgers*.

Dr Hans Kruuk has also been an inspiration and kindly allowed me to quote freely from his wide-ranging, superb research work. Prof. R.M. Anderson, Dr Paul Racey, Roger Symes and Penny Thornton all helped familiarize me with their badger research and I have made reference to other work including that of Professor Stephen Harris in Bristol. Martin

Hancox has constantly kept me informed of the continuing debates about the treatment of badgers in connection with TB and cattle, as well as all his other research work on badgers for many years. Dr Paddy Sleeman of the University of Cork has been a similar source of inspiration and encouragement for which I am more than thankful. Local knowledge on badgers has been cheerfully shared with Clive Banks and Ralph Newton over too many years to mention. I am grateful to all in the Hertfordshire Natural History Society, the Hertfordshire and Middlesex Wildlife Trust's Badger Group and all others who have accomplished so much in conservation and survey work, especially David Anderson, Brian Barton, Barbara Brady, John Card, Paul Clark, June Crew, Ron Denton, John Dietz and Helen Strojek, Roger Favell, Wayne Green, Jim and Lesley Harmer, Steve and Cathy Kourik, Andrew Martin and Helen Stevenson, Diana and Barry Norman, Keith Seaman and Emma Cooper, Barry and Rosemary Peck, Mick Robbins, Geoff Steward, Jim and Mary Sutton, Brian and Bob Smith, Shell UK, Michael, James and Judy Thody, Diana and John Wallace, Michael Wainwright, Richard Ware and Dick Last of Gilbertson and Page Ltd, David and Adrienne Watson, David Webster (DW Street Lighting), Kim Wilde, Ivor, Vaughan and Angela Williams.

Shell have sponsored a great deal of the badger project work carried out on the nature reserve for which my wife and I act as voluntary wardens and Gilpa-Valu dried dog food has been freely provided for the wildlife at the site for many years as a special form of sponsorship for the animals by Gilbertson and Page. Finally, to my wife Anna who keeps the badgers and endless other animals fed, to Susie who helps watch them and to Cathy Percival who word processed my rough notes so well, my sincere thanks.

Preface

When I first went out to survey for badgers in the early 1960s I came to one farm cottage and asked an old countryman if he knew where badgers lived near his home. He said, 'What's badgers?' and genuinely did not know of the species. I came to know of three badger colonies within a mile of where we stood, yet he never saw them. Nowadays most people, whether they live near them or not, are familiar with the black-and-white face: symbol of so many activities from organizations concerned with conservation to the youth section of the St John Ambulance Brigade.

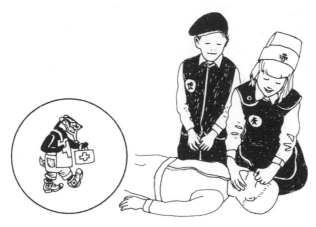

For over a hundred years the famous St John Ambulance Brigade have cared for people on a voluntary basis and they have a junior section of St John 'Badgers' for 6-10 year-olds. The black-and-white uniforms are shown as 'Badgers' practise on a mannequin with, inset, the first aid badger badge.

If we wanted a national symbol with an indigenous, indomitable and courageous species to typify all we value about our nation, what could be better than the badger? I have written an account of this animal to give the reader a wide-ranging outline of what is now known of the species without going into the depth of Dr Neal's classic works on the subject. Badgers have come in for what is known as 'a lot of media coverage' over bovine tuberculosis and the revival of badger digging has threatened the survival of these innocuous animals in some localities. I am not ashamed to have devoted a good deal of space to both themes.

Many people are making a study of badgers both at a professional and an amateur level and many more studies of badger behaviour will continue to add to our knowledge. I have included recent research into an ancient subject.

1987

Greater legal protection has been given to badgers since this book first appeared, but they are still subject to persecution and I have considerably enlarged the chapter on the legislation in this new edition. We continue to need much more research on the species.

Michael Clark 1994

Comparison of size of badger and other mammals. Left to right, roe deer, muntjac, fox, dog, cat, otter, badger, rabbit, hare and stoat.

All shapes and sizes

Although this book concentrates on the European badger *(Meles meles)*, let us put the species in its world context. Every mammal is given a genus and species name in Latin. Two or more mammals may be very similar and be grouped in the same genus; the genus is always given an initial capital letter, the species is always in lower case type. There are 9 species of badger in 7 genera within the weasel family (the Mustelidae) which altogether comprises 26 genera. Badgers are native to all the continents except Antarctica and Australasia. The closest relatives of the badgers are the weasels, polecats, mink, martens, sables, fishers, grisons, wolverines, skunks and otters, an ancient line which exploits trees, land and water. Their common ancestors are thought to be small, forest-living marten-like mammals similar to the modern ferret badgers which are much smaller and climb trees far more readily than the European species.

'You'll end up looking like that if you don't eat up all your earthworms.'

I have drawn the honey badger because it is so like ours but is classified in its own sub-family, the *Mellivora*. The rest are in six genera: *Meles* (European); *Arctonyx* (hog badgers of Asia); *Mydaus* (Indonesian stink

Honey badger (head and body: 60-70 cm, 24-30 inches.
Tail: 20-30 cm, 8-12 inches).

European badger (head and body 68-80 cm, 27-31½inches.
Tail: 12-17 cm, 5-7 inches).

Hog badger (head and body: 55-70 cm, 22-28 inches.
Tail: 12-17 cm, 5-7 inches).

Palawan stink badger (head and body: 32-46 cm, 13-18 inches.
Tail: 1-4 cm, ½-1½ inches).

Indonesian stink badger (head and body: 37-51 cm, 14½-20 inches.
Tail: 5-7 cm, 2-3 inches).

American badger (head and body: 42-72 cm, 16½-28 inches.
Tail: 10-15 cm, 4-6 inches).

Chinese ferret badger (head and body: 33-43 cm, 13-17 inches.
Tail: 15-23 cm, 6-9 inches).

badgers); *Suillotaxus* (Palawan and Calamian stink badgers); *Taxidea* (American badger); *Melogale* (ferret badgers of Asia). All this talk of 'stink', 'hog' and 'ferret' is not exactly flattering and reflects that all the badgers possess, and use to good effect, strong scent glands. The glands are used to communicate individual scent to each other, but when badgers are frightened the strong smell of musk (or worse in some species) is very noticeable and all types fluff out their tail regions in alarm. The stink badgers actually squirt the contents of their scent glands at aggressors.

All the badgers dig burrows to various degrees of complexity. Most of the other species live in simple dens when compared to the sometimes ancient and complex setts of the European species. Even the smaller American badger, which is very similar in appearance, but more carnivorous, has less permanent, simpler earths, although the stories of their digging into asphalt and even concrete roads indicate no lack of power in their limbs. Like our species, they are strong fighters and nearly half of all examined will show scars, especially around the neck, from conflicts between males. Road casualties are a major cause of deaths and peak in February/March as do those in Britain but unlike ours they are trapped for fur on a large scale with about 50,000 pelts taken every year across the USA and Canada. There is a colour variation in the north/south range of the American badger with the light facial stripe passing right down the body in the southerly types, and finishing on the nape in the northerly ones.

Facial pattern variations in Meles *across the range:* (left) *Europe;* (centre) *China and Siberia;* (right) *Manchuria, Korea and Japan. From British Museum (Natural History) skins, Long and Kondakov.*

Throughout their range, badgers have attracted persecution by men and dogs (see p.34). Their size and courage have determined the size and shape of the dogs bred. Most badgers have a distinct facial pattern which reflects an

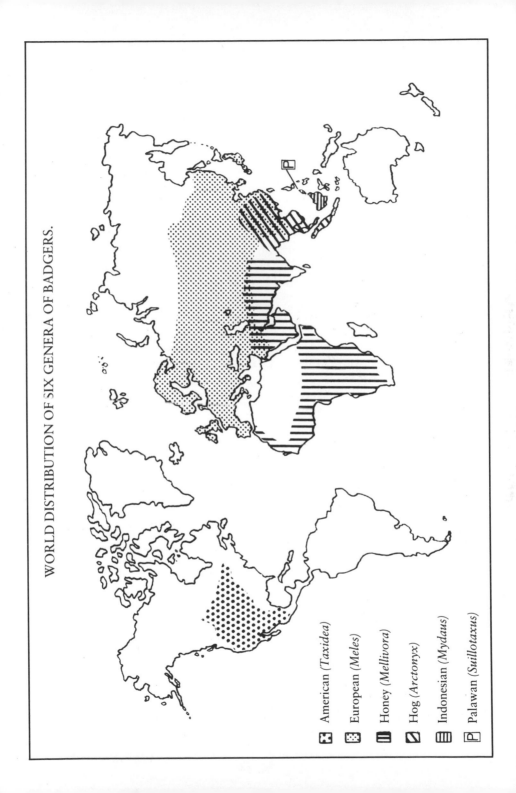

WORLD DISTRIBUTION OF SIX GENERA OF BADGERS.

American (*Taxidea*)
European (*Meles*)
Honey (*Mellivora*)
Hog (*Arctonyx*)
Indonesian (*Mydaus*)
Palawan (*Suillotaxus*)

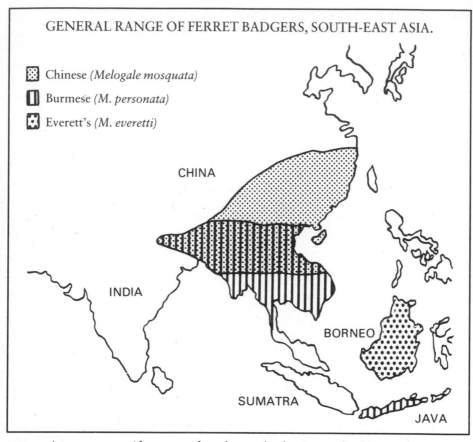

GENERAL RANGE OF FERRET BADGERS, SOUTH-EAST ASIA.

Chinese *(Melogale mosquata)*

Burmese *(M. personata)*

Everett's *(M. everetti)*

CHINA

INDIA

BORNEO

SUMATRA

JAVA

aggressive response if cornered and attacked. Honey badgers do not have these stripes, but share the large digging claws (which are immense in the Asian hog species that has been known to dig itself out of sight in a spotlight beam). Honey badgers eat scorpions, reptiles and rodents and some males specialize in catching larger mammals such as hares, foxes and aardvarks. They may also rip bark off trees to get to bee nests and dig up all types of food including buried humans. I have not come across that in British badgers, but I have known them to rip open the bark of a dead oak to eat a bee nest. Heavy flints and rocks are no obstacle when digging. Stink badgers will scratch out invertebrates of all kinds and have simple single burrows with a chamber and bedding.

To sum up: badgers are a group of mammals which have developed the work of digging to a fine art, giving security and essential protection from cold during winter in the northern types; which have very strong scent glands to maintain contact in social groups, as we will see later, to attract or warn and in some cases dramatically repel other species; which eat a wide range of foods, both animal and vegetable; which defend themselves and family to death if necessary and are persecuted for this courage by man; which are trapped, run over or poisoned by mankind throughout the world but still survive surprisingly well. All are remarkably neutral to man's economy and should be carefully protected throughout their range, whatever their variety and wherever they occur.

Badgers climb freely on play trees and will scramble up to a certain height in pursuit of food on vertical trunks. Below left, claw marks on bark; right, a chalk lump found outside a sett showing claw marks.

Badger biology

It is difficult to tell male from female badgers. Almost every night for a year I watched a heavy, distinctly pale-coloured boar which was always out feeding first; suddenly he turned up lactating and later fed with two cubs alongside! His name, recorded repeatedly in my notes as 'Old Boy' overnight turned into 'Old Girl' and I felt deservedly foolish. Boars do thicken up in the head and neck, but so do some sows, even if most are slimmer in their features, and it is safer to reserve judgement on the visual appearances until you know more about your individuals. I measured the width of the head of road casualties for many years to see if extra muscle thickness, fat deposits or skull widths gave the head greater volume in the male but could find no major differences. (The only difference I have noted in dissection arises in the growth of the sagittal crest of the skull, see p.28).

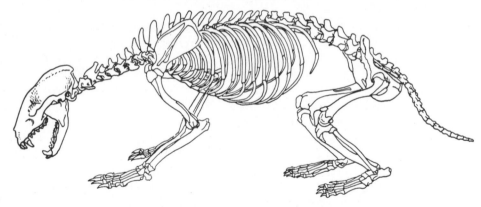

Skeleton of adult boar badger.

The coat colour is surprisingly consistent, too, apart from local ginger or, more rarely, white individuals, examples of which I have kept as skins after they were run over. Apart from these ginger-brown, ginger-red or white variations that I have observed as far apart as Hertfordshire and North Wales, the darker grey summer coat and lighter grey but thicker winter coat are very similar throughout the range. The mixture of white, yellow, brown and black in the body hairs gives a very attractive cold grey appearance. In albinos the black pigment is entirely replaced by white and the ginger specimens I have examined have been either dull brown or a distinct red

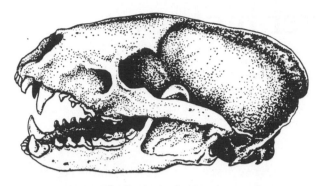

Skull of sow badger.

brown. Ginger cubs are very light, but moult into a darker brown often shared by other members of the colony. One sett I studied had a ginger boar and normal grey-coloured sow which one year produced three grey and one ginger cub.

You can sex badgers in the field if they (a) have cubs and are seen to be heavy in milk and (b) if they sit back to groom in full view of you and you can see the testes.

The male badger has an additional narrow bone in the penis, the baculum (a feature of carnivores), which is about 10cm (4 inches) long and turned up at the end. The skeleton reflects a sturdy, muscular carnivore, like the close relatives in the same weasel family, the otter, polecat and stoat. All can cope with tunnels easily and have very strong claws. I have drawn from a skinned head to show how the thick neck, head and jaw muscles surround the skull to give considerable protection. The tendency for individuals to chew and bite each other a good deal and the use of the bite in social contact, especially when a dominant individual wishes to put another badger 'in its place' or when the animal has to defend itself from attack by other carnivores (see sagittal crest section, p.28) is indicated in the number of scars around their head and neck.

Baculum or penis bone (life size) from a two-year-old male badger seen from above and side, tip on left.

The scent gland is close to the anus and glands impart scent to the faeces. There are two located just inside the anus. There is also the huge subcaudal gland which is very obvious in examination of a dead specimen. The scent it produces is so important in recognition of individuals in the social groups that badgers will mark by squatting briefly against each other and at particular places around the setts as well as in the latrines. The dominant boar tends to scent mark more than others: his scent prevails in his colony.

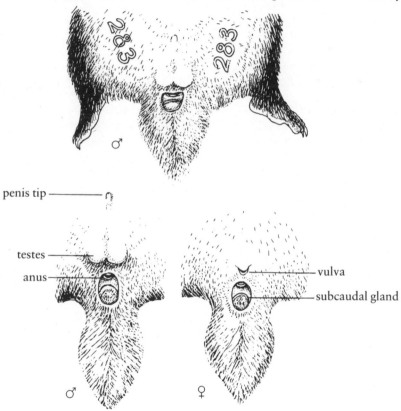

First sex your badger. When you turn a badger on its back the first thing you notice below the tail is the deep subcaudal scent gland. A sedated male badger (above) is given a permanent tattoo as well as a radio collar in research areas. The numbers show up well through the thin abdominal hair. In both sexes the anus is situated just above the subcaudal gland. The drawings (below) may look like twin bearded singers, but they are of the boar (left) with obvious testes and the tip of the penis visible well forward at the end of the baculum bone. In the sow (right) the vulva is just above the gland.

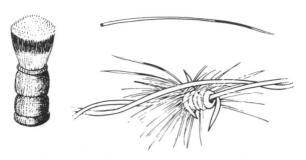
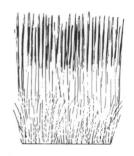

Hair today . . . millions of badger hair shaving brushes have been made and sold throughout the world over the centuries because dorsal (back) hairs have just the right degree of spring and toughness for long life. I have tried to guess how many brushes can be made from a single pelt and by bunching the hair estimate c. 10. Synthetic fibres have fortunately replaced the hair in most brushes made today, but real badger hair for expensive, posh brushes is still being imported into Britain largely from China and the Balkans. The typical long back hair of the summer coat has a white tip for about 1 cm, black for about 2 cm and yellow-white for about 4 cm amongst an underfur of 2· cm yellow-white hair. There is great variety in these proportions, from the mid-back, where the white tips are reduced to about 5 mm, to the flanks and between summer and winter coats. You most frequently find badger hairs caught on barbed wire fences where they have pushed under as they follow a path. They also occur in mud and old bedding at the entrances to setts. When hairs are rolled between finger and thumb they are distinctly coarse as if squared off and rotate in a series of bumps. Pure black hair is on the legs and stripes with lighter cream shade to white on face and ears. Musk appears to discolour the base of the tail region around the subcaudal gland to ginger. Erythristic (red) haired types and albinos lack the black (melanin) pigment.

The first teeth appear after a cub is a month old and at four months the adult set of teeth has replaced these. Tooth wear can be a good guide to age, but will vary according to the type of soil present (which gets taken in with food). Molars gradually lose the bumps that characterize all badgers, and their enamel covering over the years. (See dentition notes on p. 95)

Although badgers have a reputation for being very thick-skinned, I have found muntjac deer skin (for example) much thicker during dissection and I think it is the deep underfur, the layer of coarse hair, the fat stored under the skin and its looseness that gives a frustrating, amorphous mouthful to anything trying to bite a badger. Bites between members of the same colony or rivals frequently draw blood and we will see later (p.31) that head, neck and rump are particularly favoured in disputes.

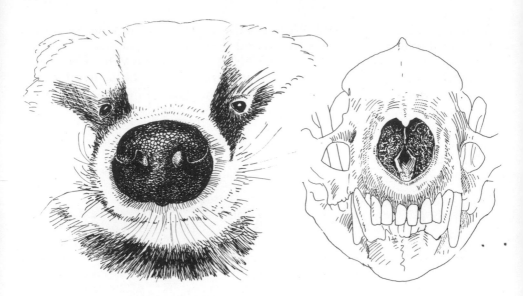

The wet, flexible nose which catches any scents on the air projects well beyond the mouth and is surrounded by sensitive whiskers. Detection of scent is more acute in moist, humid conditions and more difficult when the air and ground are dry. In the skull the complexity of the turbinals (network of tiny bones) in the olfactory cavity reflects the power of the nasal region.

The short, tough legs which excavate so well the underground home in all soil types can also dig out wasp nests buried securely underground and pull rotting trees apart with ease. The tail is short and light in colour. Any variations in colour either on face, body or around tail may well be the remains of scars after fights – when the hair grows back either dark or light. The forehead and cheeks often show bites which may scar as dark or light patches: not true variations in the body coloration.

The hairs moult into a dark, thinner summer coat; this in turn moults into a lighter-coloured coat in the autumn when considerable layers of fat are laid down under the skin. If you skin an autumn badger the contrast is striking and illustrates what considerable reserves are built up to allow the animal to survive the cold months when worms are hibernating and food might be very difficult to come by. My studies have shown that even if artificial food is made available throughout the year, when the badgers become very inactive in December the food is ignored.

The large nose is the focal point of this low-slung, animated earth mover. Everything about the badger makes it an effective digger and capable of negotiating tunnels with ease. With sensitive whiskers around the nose and above each eye, a badger lives in a world of scents. Imagine being able to smell possibly 700-800 times more than you can now and you will realize how much the air tells a badger. Many appear to set off into the wind from their sett as if making a habit of approaching places they can smell at a distance first. When feeding, the nose tests the ground and food such as earthworms carefully first. Compared with a fox they are very delicate, methodical feeders and the head is constantly in motion during feeding or searching for food.

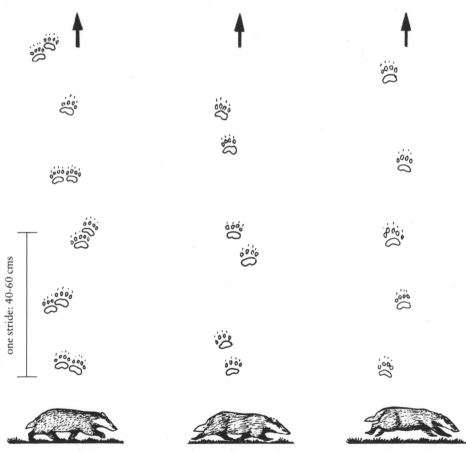

(Left to right) *Badger print patterns when walking, trotting and running fast.*

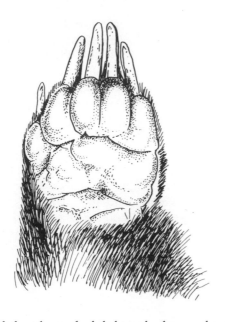

*Left fore foot of adult boar badger and typical tracks when walking in soft mud:
hind foot falling behind and on top of part of fore foot.*

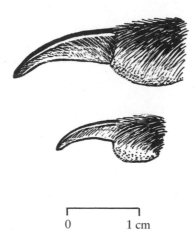

0   1 cm

*Claws on fore foot toe (above) and on a hind foot (below) to show greater size of toes
and claws on fore feet.*

The black-and-white striped face has made the badger a familiar animal to many who may never actually see one. Relatively small ears and eyes keep the outline of the body a simple tube shape with short, tough legs. The long front claws dig and may be used to defend the animal. The five toes set in front of a wide pad on each foot appear as separate marks in prints in mud, but close examination shows that they merge into the foot as one pad with only short gaps between. The pads leave unique prints that cannot be confused with any other species. Claws on the hind feet are invariably short whilst those on the front are long, unless damaged by digging.

Badgers can run very quickly in short bursts and swim well. They tunnel powerfully back and forth and regularly shuffle backwards dragging bedding to the sett. The abdominal hair is very thin in both sexes but especially so if a sow is lactating. Cubs appear to scratch at the skin when feeding and the development of their teeth must make the sows long for them to be weaned.

Dorsal view of boar in summer coat.

Side view of mature sow in winter coat.

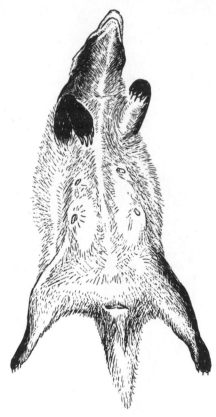

In lactation the lack of hair cover on the ventral surface is very obvious and cubs may scratch the skin.

Rear view of relaxed, walking sow in summer coat. In fright the hairs fluff up
(centre), *but in alarm* (right) *a large area stands out and hairs may erect all over the*
body in a direct confrontation. This may be found in some road casualty badgers
which have turned to face an oncoming car at the moment of death. One September
sow I have measured was 13.75 kg (30 lb) but the average autumn weight for both
sexes is around 12 kg (26 lb) and average spring weight is 9 kg (20 lb). Head and
body length is usually in the region of 73 cm (30 inches) in adults and the variable tail
is around 15 cm (6 inches) long.

Anterior view of boar in summer coat.

Development of the sagittal crest

The sagittal crest is a very obvious feature on top of the badger skull (although you cannot see it on a living badger) and develops out of the fusion of the bones above the brain case. Powerful muscles link the thick muscle tissue on either side of this ridge with the lower jaw above the hinge. One of the first things you notice about a badger skull when compaared with those of other mammals you may have examined is that the lower jaw stays locked into the sockets on either side at the base of the thick cheek bones. The muscles allow for a very powerful bite and protect the skull from these and more potentially lethal attacks by dogs or wolves. By an unhappy accident I was able to compare the development of the crests of 11-month male and female badgers run over together by the same car crossing a road. It seems likely that they were from the same litter: they had been running together, they were the same age and identical in weight at 9·5 kg (21 lb). Externally their heads appeared alike, too, apart from variations in the width of the black stripes, but I later found that the muscle and crest development were noticeably more advanced in the male. His dark red muscle pads and skull were larger and the crest well defined whereas the sow's crest had not yet developed.

The sagittal crest on the skull of a mature male badger.

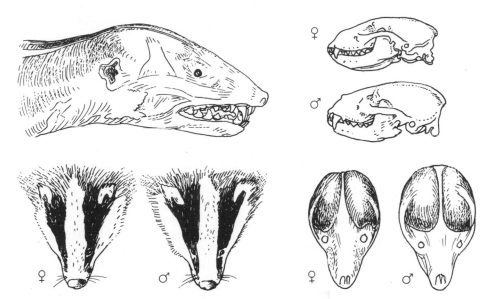

(Top left) *Head of badger showing muscles around jaws, skull and neck.*
(Top right) *Skull of eleven-month sow, above, and eleven-month boar, below.*
(Bottom left) *Eleven-month sow, left, and eleven-month boar.*
(Bottom right) *Eleven-month sow, left, showing muscles on skull and same for eleven-month boar.*

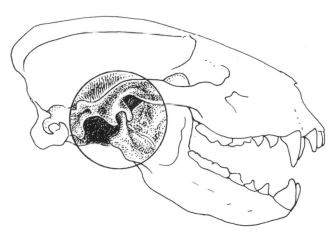

Detail of articulation of lower jaw which is locked into skull around the hinge in mature badgers.

By three or four years the mature badgers of both sexes have a deep crest and whilst this serves mostly for the attachment of the jaw muscles and neck ligaments the animal can also withstand brutal blows to the head. The defence position (see p.110) hides the sensitive nose and gives similar protection (without the spines) to that offered by a hedgehog. Stephen Kourik has shown me a skull from a dead sow road casualty where a section of the sagittal crest had been broken off but had re-grown to be partly attached once again to the rest of the crest. This may have been from a previous encounter with a vehicle. The crest and its muscles must have saved many a badger from receiving a fractured skull.

The powerful head and neck make passage effortless through the Forestry Commission two-way swing gates in plantation fencing, designed to keep out rabbits, which follow established badger paths.

Why do badgers have scars above their tails?

If it gets known that you are interested in badgers, people may be good enough to telephone you to tell you of road casualty badgers. Some local badger groups have organized collection and measurement very effectively. If you collect, measure and record the details of each one, taking care to observe the highest standards of hygiene (wearing surgical gloves in particular) you will in time come across individuals with scars over their tails. Sometimes these are quite inconspicuous, healed over with regrowth of hairs, but others are freshly cut and indicate repeated scratching or biting

Until recently the Ministry of Agriculture Fisheries and Food (MAFF) had a badger collection service to test casualties for TB.

with deep weals in the tough skin. The worst example I have seen was in a dead badger believed by the farmer to have been baited by badger diggers (who he had caught before and successfully prosecuted). It was an undersized cub of the previous year looking, at over a year old in March, the size it should have looked at five months. The rump had been savagely bitten and exposed and teeth marks suggested death was caused by a bite to the head when the badger was weak with loss of blood from the wound and unable to keep its head protected.

What happens to cause the scars I only discovered by watching at a sett where two badgers started to fight and I have subsequently witnessed two similar events. The badgers made a great deal of noise including growling, whickering and even screaming at times; the impression was of two rapidly

Whether indulging in play fighting or the real thing, badgers can move with astonishing speed and have very flexible bodies, able to twist or spin round in a split second.

rotating creatures in a frenzy, each trying to bite the tail of the other. They seemed oblivious of undergrowth as they rushed round and round through cover, across parts of a ploughed field, back through a hedge and down into the sett where even in the confined space of the tunnels the fight continued. It may be that the bites above the tail are worst when a badger is trying to escape down a tunnel because it can no longer turn round to avoid the snapping teeth. Like stags fighting with antlers which generally interlock to avoid giving mortal injuries in fights, badgers seem to attack the least vital area of the body – the thick rump. (The badger mentioned which died from a head wound was a rare example.) The spinning movement is created by each one going for the tail of the other but trying at the same time to keep its own rump away from the adversary. In the days following the three fights I have witnessed in every case a new sett entrance was dug on the perimeter of the main sett – or annexe sett – area as if the weaker animal has had to move out of the family group but is still tolerated at night when feeding with the group as long as it uses a different retreat in the daytime. When I was in contact with the late Viscount Knutsford about badger setts in his fox-hunting districts he wrote about finding badgers with scars: 'In my long experience, if I have found a single hole in an unusual place for badgers it has been occupied by a badger of either sex with a sore place just above the tail. I sent one of these skins to *The Field* and was rewarded by the stupid remark that it was some form of "skin infection". Whatever it is, it seems to cause the badgers to move into solitude.'

The observation gives valuable field evidence that after what may have been frequent fights, badgers can be ostracized from family groups and live in isolation, certainly for a time, perhaps until they are accepted back under a change of circumstances.

In one case I watched a recently bitten sow hold back and wait until all but one of a group of six had finished feeding. As it approached, the last remaining badger confronted the latecomer and bit it on the neck. There was only a passive response and no fight developed which indicated that the individual accepted a clear pecking order or position in the social group.

Badgers and the good old days

You must have heard the expression 'badgering' or used it yourself in connection with someone who bullies, or relentlessly pesters someone. Badgers are part of our language because of the brutal way we have trapped, dug up and teased them with dogs throughout the centuries. Ernest Neal records Harting's suggestion that the name 'badger' was derived from 'becheur', the French for 'digger'.

In medieval Britain, taverns became centres for the backyard activity of baiting and Turner noted in 'All heaven in a Rage' that captured badgers, sometimes baited in bear pits, were taken to Smithfield where 'the scum of the metropolis gathered' according to Henry Alken in *British Field Sports*. Publicans encouraged the activity, which drew crowds and therefore increased sales of ale. Bets were laid on how many times a terrier could draw the badger from a box or artificial tunnel. Some badgers recorded in the nineteenth-century magazine *Sports and Pastimes* had their tails nailed to the ground and were baited until they died either from injuries or from a gangrenous tail. This indicates how prolonged the ordeals could be; eventually the first official attempt to ban baiting of bulls, bears and badgers was made in 1800. There was great resistance in Parliament and Windham, Secretary at War, opposed it by saying that baiting had existed for over a thousand years and as a schoolboy he had attended two bull baits and did not think his character had suffered. (That sounds familiar, does it not?) The bill was defeated and *The Times* vigorously supported Windham. Richard Martin, one of the earliest animal campaigning MPs, worked to gradually gain support for Bills to stop bull-, bear- and badger-baiting and the sports of dog fighting and (would you believe) monkey fighting. The history of reform in the treatment of animals is long and fascinating and suffice it to say it was not until 1835 that it became illegal to bait badgers. Even then there was great opposition and today the practice continues amongst some particularly perverted people, in secret, as with dog fighting and cock fighting.

Mortimer-Batten, an early author on badgers, noted in 1923 that in the past, baiting had been the price of badgers' existence. It is an interesting point and may show that although the species did not fit into the field sport chase of fox and otter, this large animal was preserved for such unpleasant activities, despite all the trapping and digging. Clearly people 'left' certain

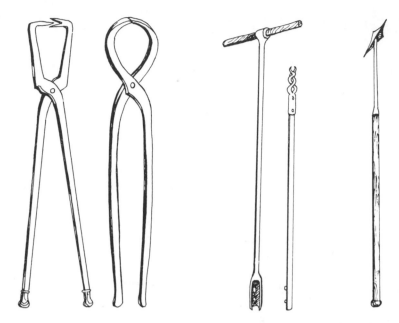

As well as long narrow spades, blacksmiths would fashion tongs for badger diggers to a variety of designs (two examples on left) and listening rods were often used to mark more accurately where terrier and badger were arguing below ground. Some could be fitted with ear trumpets on the end to amplify the barking and growling. Digging would commence as close to where the noise was coming from as possible. Like the spears used by otter hunters, an evil harpoon spike (far right) was used up to 1.75 m (6 foot) along a tunnel on a flexible rod to bend round corners. Impaled in the badger, the rod would be twisted to lock into the skin and then drawn out along with the struggling animal. Jocelyn Lucas describes the use of the tongs in his Hunt and Working Terriers (1931):

'If the badger is facing the dog, it requires an experienced and sagacious terrier to do this job properly. My old dog "Ilmer Jack" used to wait his opportunity, and then get either the cheek or the forehead. In neither case could the badger bite back.

'When tailing a badger, it is necessary to whip him off the ground quickly and to keep him well clear of your legs or he'll get you!

'When bagging him, the best way is to tail him, and then get someone to put the tongs round his neck, and use them to guide him into the sack. Otherwise, whoever is holding the mouth of the sack is liable to get bitten, for the badger has no desire to go in it. If a terrier has hold of him (it will be by the head if he has!), you can use him instead of the tongs. Someone must lift the dog, and someone else the badger—by the tail. Drop the badger in the sack, bringing the mouth up to the dog's muzzle and then close it. The dog's head is outside, of course, and he must let go in a moment or so, for he won't be able to breathe if he doesn't, and in any case once he can't see the badger he'll let go quicker.

'Don't beat the wretched dog to make him let go, and don't let any other dogs loose at the time. Any that are loose will be quite uncontrollable. As soon as you have the badger in his sack, hang it on the limb of a tree. For one thing the badger can breathe better, and he's sure to be blown, and for another he's liable to eat his way out if he's on the ground.

'Badger clubs generally have special sacks made of strong material, and furnished with eyelets for ventillating purposes, as well as a strap and buckle at the neck. The badger can get his nose through to breathe, but the metal eyelet stops him from doing more.'

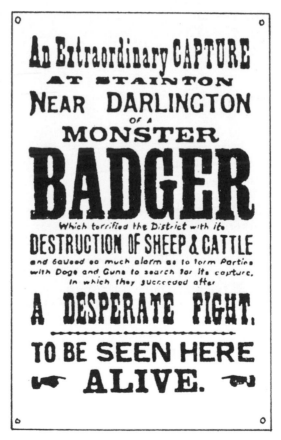

A 1911 (yes, 1911, not 1711) poster at Leyburn Wensleydale annual fair where a half-grown badger fed on fish was exhibited with several guinea pigs.

badger earths where they laid up during daylight as long as they did not upset the fox hunters, for the purpose of obtaining badgers to bait at a later date. Some of the setts became huge fortresses and one in my own county of Hertfordshire was first recorded over 200 years ago when men tried to dig out badgers over ten days in pure chalk yet failed to capture even one. The sett survives to this day. He wrote of baiting:

An amusing anecdote is told in the locality of Hutton-le-Hole concerning a badger drawing test which took place some years ago, and which, as usual, smelt of beer and pigsties. The badger was in the ordinary type of rectangle wooden box, and the owner of it offered bets of two to one that no dog present could get it out. With becoming bashfulness a ruddy-faced farm labourer, the owner of a long-bodied, long-haired sheep dog whelp stepped up and accepted the bet. It goes without saying that the badger was not new to the game, and that his owner's confidence was the result of many similar meetings.

The ground was cleared, and the farm labourer introduced his cur to the mouth of the hole, 'ticing' him on with befitting sounds. The cur was not interested, so the man got hold of him and shoved him down the hole, tail first. A howl from the dog signified that the badger had obtained a good grip, whereupon the youth let go, and the dog shot out of the artificial earth with the badger still fast to his hind-quarters! So the youth won his bet.

To anyone conversant with the habits and history of this beast, he stands out as rather a pathetic figure; but little is to be gained by dwelling upon this unhappy phase of his life. The badger is a friendly and lovable beast. That he is not usually pictured as such is because he is most generally seen under unhappy conditions – perhaps as a cornered and terrified victim, filled with suspicion at his surroundings, and dreading attack. Fortunately, the badger never realizes that his case is hopeless. I have known a starving and broken-hearted beast, after days of captivity and misery, to fight as gamely for its life as when first taken from its home, and, so long as a badger lives, its tenacity never wavers no matter how dark the prospects.

We humans have not changed our characters so much as adapted our behaviour nowadays. Competitive sport between people has fortunately replaced hunting for most of the world's population. All the skills of throwing spears are ritualized into bowling a cricket ball, for example, and the competitive chase and excitement of football exercise the same

(Left to right) *After Ernest H. Shepard in* The Wind in the Willows *by Kenneth Grahame (Methuen, 1931); Alfred Bestall in* Rupert *(Express Newspapers, 1946); Beatrix Potter in* The Tale of Mr Tod *(Warne, 1912); Mr Tod is the old country name for a fox: Tommy Brock was the badger's name in the story.*

(Top) *After Thomas Bewick (1785); (centre left) perhaps my favourite drawing of all of a badger, after J.G. Millais (1905); (centre right) Eileen Soper in* When Badgers Wake *(Routledge and Kegan Paul, 1955); (bottom) Eunice Overend in* Badgers without bias *(Abson, 1981).*

American versions: (top) *after John James Audubon (1848);* (centre) *Ernest Thompson Seton (1909);* (bottom) *detail of John Schoenherr's illustration in* Incident at Hawk's Hill *by Allan W. Eckert (Little, Brown, Toronto, 1971).*

characteristics as pursuing hares and rabbits. Badgers would not run in the manner of a fox and be chased so that, as we have seen, they remained on the side-lines as far as field sports were concerned. Ironically by their stubborn courage they epitomized all that was finest in our own human characters. In our children's literature, Kenneth Grahame gave a delightful and informed view of the species in *Wind in the Willows* (1908). He tells of how man (probably the Romans) had built on the very site of the wild wood, but then left. 'It is their way,' said Badger. 'But we remain. There were badgers here, I've been told, long before that same city ever came to be. And there are badgers here again. We are an enduring lot, and we may move out for a time, but we wait, and are patient, and back we came. And so it will ever be.' Beatrix Potter did not really seem to like the species very much (see the *Tale of Mr Tod*) but Bestall gave him an important role as Rupert Bear's best friend, Bill.

Our language has adopted two names for the species: 'brock' from the Celtic *broc* and 'badger', if not from 'digger' probably from 'badge' or 'stripe' because of the distinctive facial pattern. 'Brock' survives as a common alternative name and there are place names which refer to the presence of badgers in most areas. I was born near Broxbourne ('Badgers' Brook') in Hertfordshire, where the local Borough Council has taken on the characteristic badger mask for their logo, and the firm of Tesco, which has its headquarters nearby, has probably the most spectacular badger coat of arms in existence.

'And why on earth should you wish to come to Broxbourne School?'

'Gentlemen, our takeover bid for Fox's Glacier Mints has succeeded!'

'And here are some of our other relatives: top left, the Brookes of Wexham Park; top right, the Brokes of Holme-Hale; bottom left, the Brocklehursts of Sudeley Castle and finally the Fitsherbert-Brockholes of Cloughton.'

After the first edition of this book appeared I received a framed print of a Barry Driscoll painting commissioned by Tescos of two animated badgers in a landscape which now hangs in public view at my place of work in North Hertfordshire College. The Duke of Edinburgh saw the coat of arms when on a visit to Tescos and said that badgers do not often appear like that (or words to that effect). The painting was produced and sent to the Palace to show the species in its true light and a limited edition of prints were made. I can now also confirm that the headmaster of Broxbourne School does not resemble my drawing, on p. 40, either.

The magnificent work *Burke's Landed Gentry* (my 1939 edition has 3,058 pages) illustrates a number of coats of arms with badgers prominent. 'Brockholes', 'Brooke', 'Broke' and 'Brocklehurst', for example, are all old family names derived from badgers.

Tall, silent types?

Badgers are not generally thought of as being very vocal animals, but they have a range of sounds to suit most occasions even if these are more reminiscent of the traditions of Madonna than of Pavarotti, as you might say. They will purr, growl, snarl, whicker, scream, yelp and grunt, particularly when at play, mating, wrestling, biting, chewing ears or necks, leap-frogging, mutual grooming or fighting. They eat noisily with much smacking of lips. They probably even mutter to themselves about the problems of earthmoving when digging. The whicker is familiar to badger-watchers and is not unlike the pleasant sounds of communication between horses in a stable, but the cries of anger or pain during a full blown fight are unhappy sounds indeed.

Badger diet

Badgers live in colonies, but generally feed alone, although they may meet and search for food close to each other in the best areas on a particular night. They are happy to eat earthworms *(Lumbricus terrestris* especially) night after night – rather like a continuous diet of spaghetti Bolognese for you and me.

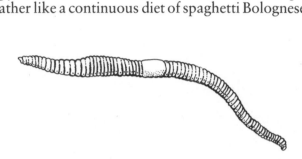

The earthworm, Lumbricus terrestris, *at the basis of badger social life as well as their diet. Life size for average worm.*

When I was first interested in badgers and collected road casualties I quickly found that those run over after feeding in pastures would have as many as a hundred worms in their stomachs. These pass through the digestive system quickly and an adult badger likes about twice that number to see it through a good day's sleep. If you go out on a still, wet summer night (worms shun cold nights) and look for worms on the surface of short grass, you realize how difficult it is to creep up on them. Any vibration or sudden flash of torchlight and they will shrink away back into the ground, retracting into their tunnels with a quick contraction of their muscles. The worms usually anchor themselves in their tunnels for this rapid retreat, but they will risk all to move onto the open grass to mate. Badgers, unlike us, walk across grass with their highly sensitive noses and mouths within a centimetre or two of the worms. Even on all fours a human cannot duplicate this proximity to the ground.

The worm casts you see in grassland or recently ploughed land in spring and autumn are the undigested soil and plant material passed by two large worm species, which are less favoured by badgers: *Allolobophora nocturna* and *A. longa.* These species tend to remain below ground all summer in the soil whereas *Lumbricus* not only emerge all the year round if warm enough, but lie on the surface on mild, damp nights. They wrap themselves in a mucus

'sleeping bag' secreted around their bodies by their saddles during mating. This temporary immobility gives badgers an even better chance of capturing them. On one occasion when a warm, still night after wet weather ended with a sudden frost just before dawn I found moribund worms including mated pairs in pasture by a sett. The combination of these conditions is rare, but I was able to walk round at first light and find in which parts of the farmland near the sett the worms had been active that night. There were large numbers on a sheltered slope (north facing, oddly enough), yet none on a higher, more exposed pasture nearby. Badgers must become expert at locating where the worms are active on a particular night. Conditions can change by the hour as the wind alters direction quite suddenly and experienced badgers will hunt accordingly. Much of their feeding may appear haphazard but modern studies with night-viewing binoculars have suggested that badgers make for the appropriate feeding grounds to suit the conditions they find when they emerge. Foxes do not compete directly for food with badgers, but they have been known to follow badgers to places where worms are prevalent.

Because each segment in a worm's body is a separate compartment mostly filled with water, badgers receive enough moisture without drinking water as long as worms form a large part of the night's food. The soil and leaves that remain when the flesh is digested give badger droppings their soft, muddy character, not unlike a very large worm cast. There are four pairs of bristles, or chaetae, to every body segment of *Lumbricus* and these worms belong to the class Chaetopoda, named after their tiny hairs. The chaetae allow earthworms to move by body contractions and also keep them securely fixed in the ground when searching for leaves or other worms above ground. The bristles are not digested by badgers when they eat them and can be found by microscopic examination of their faeces. An acre of good pasture may support 100,000 worms but at a guess weather conditions are only likely to allow a badger to eat some 20,000 worms in a whole year, throughout its territory (see p.65). Worms may live for a decade, but it takes two years for the young worms to mature.

If you watch badgers feeding through image intensifiers you will see how some worms are whipped up quickly, followed by a sharp snap by the badger to get the whole worm in the mouth. When a worm has anchored itself in the ground, the badger is careful not to tug at the long, extended body. This would result in too many breakages, which are wasteful, and also result in grit coming out of the worm, in the mouth, which is also a strong deterrent. Several worms may be taken every minute in very favourable conditions. Damp woodlands also allow capture amongst the ground flora and on paths. In fact well trodden badger paths provide 'lures' for worms as do moles' tunnels which become natural traps for worms which tumble through the

Badgers can capture earthworms most easily on short, well cropped pasture.

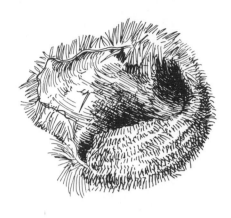

Hedgehogs, left (found as carrion, injured or caught unawares and pulled open), are cleaned down to the spines with all else consumed. Adult rabbits (myxomatosis victims usually) are skinned inside out, leaving stomach and caecum as a rule.

sides. Paths expose unsuspecting victims to the passing badger.

Even when earthworms are available our 'opportunistic omnivore' will take many other foods and I have found a bank vole amongst the earthworms in the stomach contents of a road casualty badger. Field voles are the most frequent type of vole taken, especially those caught at nests with juveniles, but mice, rats, moles, shrews, hedgehogs and rabbits, particularly young in stops (nursery tunnels) are also eaten. Insects are caught all through the year and you will often see holes in pasture where cockchafer beetle larvae have been dug up. Adult beetles are relished and cowpats turned over or dug apart to get at the dung beetles. Daddy-long-legs or crane flies are eaten as larvae or adults as they hatch in summer.

Wasps' nests are dug out for the grubs and once I watched all summer next to a sett was not excavated until September when the colony was at its peak population. A badger path went past the nest and I am sure they must have known of the insects all through the summer. These wasps were particularly aggressive and I could only photograph them by remote control having put on all my beekeeping gear to approach with the tripod. (The flashguns I found later had stings left on them.) I also tried to approach at night when I thought the nest would be quiet, but I still had to retreat when three or four wasps chased me off. The badger or badgers took two nights to complete the job: parts of the nest and many adults were left at first, but the large chamber was empty after 48 hours. They seem able to cope with all the stings and bumble bees, wild bees and very occasionally hive bees are attacked for the

Bemused wasps around their partly destroyed nest. Badgers may finish the job over a second night. Wasp grubs are a favourite summer food.

honey. Almost any other insect food may be picked up, some birds and their eggs, especially under large roosts or nest sites, may be eaten, along with frogs, toads, slugs, snails and carrion, but cereals are much more common, especially wheat and oats which are on so many farms. As the harvests are taken in, autumn fruits will have commenced, and blackberries, yew berries, strawberries, apples, pears, plums, acorns, pig-nuts and fungi are enjoyed at times. I once found my favourite edible fungi, morells, scratched up with grass and partly eaten by a sett entrance. I confess I pinched them to finish off at home (in case they were forgotten and allowed to rot).

Our diagram shows that badgers have an omnivorous, very mixed diet with the humble worm at its base. In fact, social life and territorial structure are determined by earthworms. Ernest Neal summed it all up by saying that a whole philosophy can be built on the simple truth that life is about relationships and we will see how Hans Kruuk uses the Scottish clan system to describe how animal societies are organized in response to their environment.

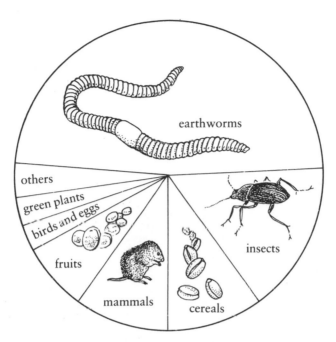

Relative frequency of major food items through the year. Every year is different, and cereals, for example, will replace worms in droughts for several weeks.

Do badgers and foxes compete for food?

Although both badgers and foxes share many items of food, their diets do not bring them into real competition during normal conditions. Badgers favour earthworms and other invertebrates when available, whereas the first choice of rural foxes is small mammals. Good worming conditions will provide more than enough food for both species on warm, still, damp nights. If badgers sniff out vole, mouse or rabbit nests on rough pasture or along field edges, they are not likely to seriously reduce the numbers available to the skilful hunting foxes. Only when all types of food are in very short supply (in prolonged droughts especially) could a large population of badgers and foxes have any significant effect on each other and cubs of either species may then die. There is, therefore, seldom actual rivalry between the two and fights to the death are rare. Only in the artificial situation in gardens where both are fed by householders and argue over food put out for them will you see frequent squabbles as they queue up to approach the meal. Both are omnivorous and in the autumn abundance of berries there are invariably soft fruits for all. In urban habitats which are much more frequently penetrated by foxes than by badgers, foxes scavenge for over half their food in some districts. They also cache (bury in secret) food when it is surplus to their immediate requirements, but badgers are not known to do this. Perhaps badgers occasionally benefit from this by sniffing out buried morsels and eating them.

You might like to see if badgers and foxes compete to take up residence in an artificial sett if you have an old shed adjoining badger country. A clear viewing top to the box inside the shed and curved pipes to keep out the light will work for both species. Above view shows pipes before soil is replaced.

When is a sett not a sett?

The focus of the life of a badger colony is their underground home called the sett, but if you go looking for a sett you will find a confusing variety of holes to choose from. The most common burrows are those of rabbits and although these mammals are less than a quarter of the size of badgers and their holes are correspondingly smaller than badgers', they like the same well

Old, very active sett entrances as here (seen from below) are easy to recognize by their huge spoil heaps, but smaller, new holes can be similar to rabbit earths. Look for clues around the entrance as well as checking its size. Rabbit droppings may not rule out the presence of badgers. Note here bedding, skull, lumps of chalk with claw marks, scratched tree trunk and large paths.

drained banks, easily worked soils and foliage cover around the holes where they live.

When rabbits excavate soil from their burrows the activity generally results in a spoil heap of small particles from their scratching paws; badgers leave larger lumps. This is particularly obvious in chalk, but heaps of sand outside a hole look much the same whichever species has been active; the quantity of soil is a good guide. This can be immense in the case of badger colonies which have been established in the same place over many years and the spoil sometimes looks like a part of the slope or hillside from which it was excavated. Foxes and rabbits may use parts of badger setts so that a close inspection of an entrance is needed to find signs of which animals are in occupation.

Look first at the shape and size of the hole. It must continue back into the ground between 200 mm (8 inches) and 300 mm (12 inches) from roof to tunnel floor. Most rabbit holes are between 150 mm (6 inches) and 200 mm (8 inches) wide at the entrance, but this will vary according to the history of interference by larger predators. Weasels, stoats, polecats and ferrets will not generally enlarge rabbit burrows during investigations for the occupants, but dogs, foxes, badgers and men with spades will do.

Most badger setts in woodland will show exposed tree roots in the entrances and some holes take on the near perfect symmetry of the badger's curved back. The entrances usually dip down and then up as they disappear from view. This must help drain water away in very wet weather. Sand and chalk are the most popular soils and will be selected in mixed clay and chalk or clay and gravel areas. First look for large lumps of the local stone or chalk on the heap. Badgers are very strong and can dig out large flints, for example, way beyond the resources of a rabbit. Old bedding (see p.57) which gets cleared out of the sett regularly tends to become matted into the soil and the cleaned out droppings from underground latrines used in the winter can be found as hard 'fossil' dung where all moisture has been lost and the effect is similar to the results of modern freeze-drying techniques of small animals by taxidermists. Where sand overlays clay you frequently find balls of clay with badger hairs rolled into the soil. (The second only colour picture I ever took of a badger was of one backing out of a sandy sett rolling clay between its fore feet. The clay appears to be cleaned from the body – hence the hairs – and then removed onto the spoil.) The irritation of wet clay in grooming may be as relevant to badgers in their preference of other soils as the ease of drainage and digging. Clay would tend to hold the water in the sett and keep the air and bedding damp.

An occupied sett should show easily recognizable footprints (see p.23) around the opening and badger hairs trodden into the soil. Rabbit hairs are soft and short compared with the longer, coarse, banded hairs of badgers. Fox hairs – from the back at least – are also softer and redder than back hairs of badgers. Even ginger badger hairs are quite different in texture from fox.

Badger setts come in different sizes and one sett does not equal one social group. Some groups of holes are extensive, sometimes just one hole is found. Both would qualify for the term 'sett'. This is all very confusing, but Penny Thornton came up with a useful definition during her badger research at Exeter University dividing setts into four types:

1   *The main sett*, which has a number of entrances, used and disused, with large spoil heaps. Always active and with well used paths. Only one main sett per social group.

2   *Annexe setts*, which also have many well used entrances and worn paths to the main sett, 50-150 m (55-160 yards) away. Not, however, always in use.

3   *Subsidiary setts* with variable number of entrances and not connected to other setts by obvious paths. Not always in use.

4   *Outlier setts* with 1, sometimes 2 holes and no defined path. Only sporadically used.

It would be helpful if these definitions became standard for all survey and study work.

As we stand outside the entrances to setts, whatever their size, it would be tempting to 'do a Bellamy' and shrink down enough to see round the whole system of tunnels and sleeping chambers. Fibre optics have made this a more possible as well as a safer option and research has been done in plotting excavated setts. A much published plan of a Gloucestershire sett shows how entrances lead back into random blind tunnels and a maze of linking routes between chambers where bedding is found. The tunnels have clearly been developed by generations of badgers as they extended their living quarters and the sleeping areas appear to be enlarged sections of tunnel rather than clearly defined 'rooms'. Dung is left in various discreet corners of the complex. The sett excavated by MAFF staff had 94 tunnels, a total of 310 m (340 yards) in length and sometimes went nearly 2 m (6 feet) below ground.

On hillsides, setts can be very deep in their furthest recesses. In the MAFF surveyed hedgerow sett 25 tonnes of soil had been dug, scratched back through the tunnels and thrown out through the entrances to be dispersed onto the spoils outside.

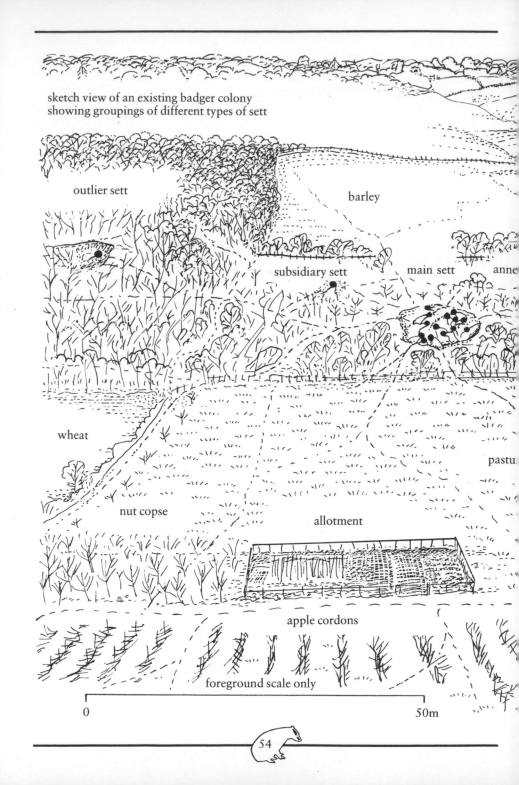

sketch view of an existing badger colony
showing groupings of different types of sett

outlier sett

barley

subsidiary sett

main sett

anne

wheat

pastu

nut copse

allotment

apple cordons

foreground scale only

0

50m

54

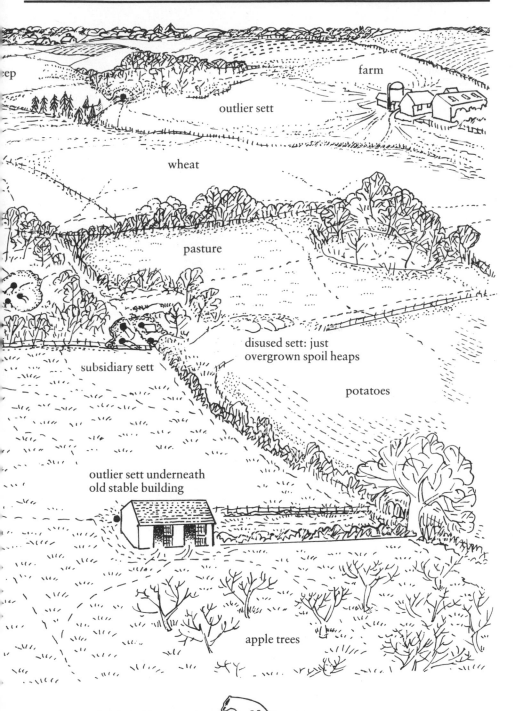

ep

farm

outlier sett

wheat

pasture

disused sett: just
overgrown spoil heaps

subsidiary sett

potatoes

outlier sett underneath
old stable building

apple trees

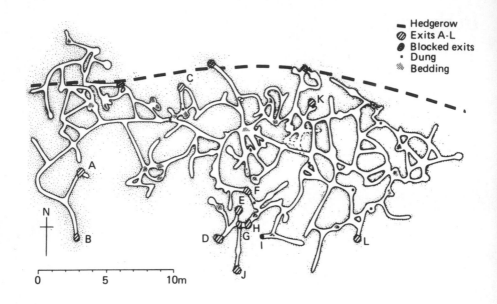

Plan of a large sett in Gloucestershire (by courtesy of the Ministry of Agriculture, Fisheries and Food).

When you look for setts in a new area (which may be in a hedge, pit, copse, open field or even canal bank or garden) you can often guess where the badgers have lived. In a wood, for example, it helps if you can get a distant view from above. This is possible in hilly country, which is the most favoured by the species. Look for elder in the tree canopy because this relatively small but very vigorous species thrives on the disturbed soil around setts. Badgers love the low cover it provides which gives them security as they emerge from below ground. A patch of elder or more scrub-like foliage will probably point to an old pit in the wood where chalk or sand has been exposed and the badgers have colonized the well drained banks. Your first clue to their presence might be the latrines (see p. 67) and distinct paths. Paddy Sleeman has also come up with a connection between the presence of stinkhorn fungi *(Phallus impudicus)* and the sites of badger setts (see p. 68).

Sett surveys are an exciting and enjoyable way of exploring the countryside, but always get permission to stray off footpaths or bridleways. You can learn so much from meeting local landowners, as long as you approach them in the right way.

In the right sett

Badgers are known to regularly share their setts with foxes, rabbits and, abroad, porcupines. I have watched many a wood mouse exit from sett entrances as well and picked up the best polecat-ferret I ever had from one. A stoat chased a rabbit into a sett where I was waiting one day and clearly knew the galleries well. They eventually ran off across a field. Dr Neal has compiled a list of mammals which also share the earths on a temporary basis: as well as those mentioned they are bank voles, brown rats, pine martens, polecats, weasels, feral cats, wild cats and, abroad, racoons, stone martens and wolves.

Bedding

Badgers take great trouble over gathering bedding, which is a vital insulation for them inside the sett tunnels in winter. They become so preoccupied with dragging material back to the sett that the noise may smother the sound of a human footfall. As long as you are downwind of them, this is one time you can stalk right up to a badger. Dry material is essential, although you sometimes see green garlic leaves, bluebells and fresh grass taken into the sett entrance. Straw

Up to her eyes in work, a sow shuffles backwards using her chin and fore feet to drag the dry bedding into her sett.

is preferred, but grass and hay is freely scratched up. Rolled heaps of bedding are frequently left on paths or under hedgerows; perhaps in such cases the badger was disturbed, distracted or just got bored with collecting after several trips. It is a major activity in suitable weather conditions when not hunting for earthworms. The furthest I have known bedding collected was 130 m (142 yards) from the sett; a trail of hay had been left, and then the hay had been rolled up by the field as the badger backed under a fence, into old apple cordons and across a field to a path in a wood to the sett. Interestingly, it had kept to cover rather than shuffle backwards in a direct line. Bedding around holes may be freshly forgotten, rejected, old, cleaned out or accidentally brought out with soil during digging. It usually includes badger hairs and may yield ectoparasites (such as fleas and lice). An interesting experiment is to leave straw with orange binder twine near a sett to see when it re-appears. (Longest known underground: 14 months.) I have filled a trailer with straw and left it at sett holes and had nearly the whole load taken below ground within 24 hours during a cold spell in January. This could actually help a colony in prolonged periods of freezing weather.

Distribution

My map (opposite) was originally prepared for Dr Neal's book on badgers (published by Croom Helm) based on records compiled by Clem Clements for the Mammal Society and is shown here by their kind permission. Further surveys have concentrated on selected areas and an estimate of some 30,000 main setts (where badgers spend most of their time) seems about right. This suggests a population of around 150,000 individual badgers nationally.

DISTRIBUTION OF BADGER SETTS (OCCUPIED AND UNOCCUPIED) IN ENGLAND, SCOTLAND AND WALES. AFTER E.D. CLEMENTS.

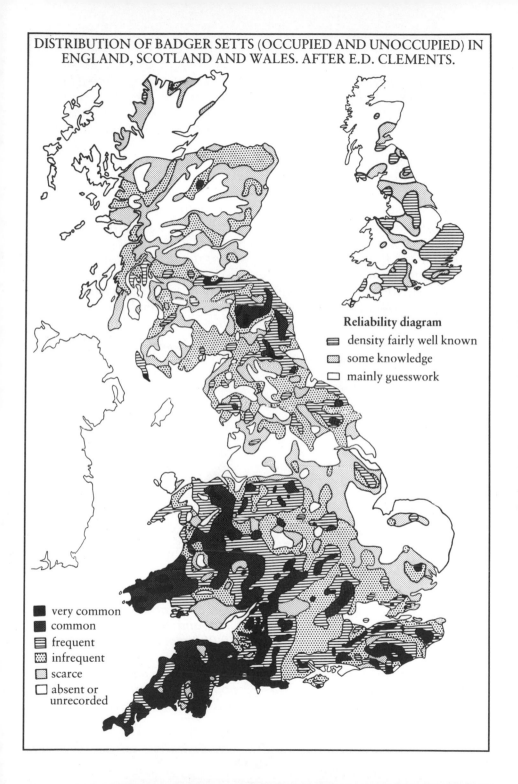

Reliability diagram
- ☰ density fairly well known
- ▨ some knowledge
- ☐ mainly guesswork

- ■ very common
- ■ common
- ☰ frequent
- ▦ infrequent
- ▨ scarce
- ☐ absent or unrecorded

Is anyone at home?

The old method of seeing if an earth is occupied was to put sticks across the hole. If these had been knocked to one side during the night, you could tell that an animal had used the entrance, but if there is one way to guarantee making badgers nervous and unpredictable, putting sticks across their sett entrances must be it. I do not recommend this or any interference round badger setts which leaves scent and frightens them. I devised a method with adhesive tape and sticks which is illustrated and causes a minimum of disturbance. It has the advantage of showing what species has used the entrance because hairs are stuck to the tape, and, from its angle next day, an idea of whether the animal had emerged or just looked in can be gained. I have known a tape to be so twisted and covered in hairs I swear the badger stopped to rub its back on it as it came out. The transparent edge must look little different from a spider's web and if you push the sticks holding the tape into the soil early in the day, no scent should be left around. Split bamboo cane dyed green as used in gardens is ideal. One disadvantage is that heavy rain can detach the gum from the tape. Why not just watch from a safe distance and see where the badgers come from!

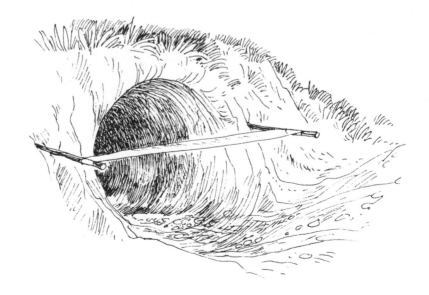

Badger territories

We know that badgers live in setts and stay together as a social group, but why should this be? Until quite recently the way badgers behaved towards each other was little understood. Modern techniques of marking individuals and following them at night have transformed our knowledge of badgers, thanks to people like Hans Kruuk and Chris Cheeseman. Both had experience of working in Africa on different pack-living carnivores and I recommend the reader to Kruuk's hyena books and the more recent *Cry of the Kalahari* by Mark and Delia Owens who have taken studies of the brown hyenas to a very advanced stage. Why talk about hyenas in a book on badgers? Because carnivore territories are such fascinating reflections of the lives of the animals and a comparison of the two types can explain much.

Kruuk, who always gives entertaining as well as highly scientific papers to the Mammal Society, came to study badgers from work on spotted hyenas and used the Scottish clan system as a way of describing carnivore social groups: clan size was directly related to the size of territory and the geography of Scotland. The fertile east had many clans in small territories, whereas the harsh, mountainous west Highlands resulted in large individual clans to match the massive but impoverished tracts of land. Human and animal (including badger) societies are both organized in response to their environment. Kruuk noted that the 220 or more species of modern carnivores, which hunted alone in some cases or in packs in others, had evolved from a solitary genet-like ancestor. All 7 families of these carnivores have 1 or 2 species that have come to live in colonies. The badger is our British example of the Mustelidae, which, like hyenas, have found that co-operation pays dividends. The Owens found in the Kalahari that even the 'solitary' brown hyena turned out to have common dens for the young and did at times share food. If a mother died, other related hyenas would keep the young alive. This is what is known as 'kin selection', where cousins feed young especially if their mother has died to ensure survival so that their genes are passed on to future generations. The Owens witnessed up to five brown hyenas on a kill in the wet season, but found them solitary when food became scarce and limited to small prey in the dry season. They found behaviour such as neck biting, pecking orders and scent marking, very like the behaviour of our badgers; however, they also recorded honey badgers killed by lions when food was very short – something very different from here, where modern badgers have no enemies except man. The still rather

Badger masks and fur may be made into sporrans (large pouch purses) worn in the Highlands, badger masks are printed on Wildlife Trust ties, moulded into buttons and carved in walking stick handles. Some hunters wear a badger baculum as a tie pin and diggers have been known to have buttons made of badger teeth on their waistcoats.

mysterious movements of our badgers from sett to sett in spring and late summer or autumn, whilst clearly related to mating behaviour, have links with lions where the Owens noted that, although males usually take over female prides, females were able to move into other territories to mix with different social groups and then leave after mating.

Both hyenas and badgers defend a carefully scent-marked area of ground around their homes, the territory, within which there may be several setts, but whilst spotted hyenas hunt together to obvious advantage, why should badgers live together, but then usually disappear into the night to feed alone?

A badger squats briefly against a stone by a sett entrance to mark with scent (or 'musk') from the subcaudal gland. Badgers scent mark each other frequently, too, especially the dominant boar on his colony. To us the fatty secretions have a pleasant, musky aroma.

In fact studies have shown that badgers were using the same feeding places at different times of the night within the territory. Badgers caught and sedated within 4 minutes by ketamine hydrochloride could be measured, sexed, weighed and fitted with a beta light, collar and transmitter. The ecologists licensed to do this work could thus find who sleeps where and with whom. (So be careful if you ever wake up fitted with a beta light and transmitter round your neck.) They found that badgers move from sett to sett but only rarely do they stray into a neighbouring territory. If they then meet an incumbent a fierce fight is likely.

In other studies, small plastic markers have been put in food, a colour for each sett, and the markers have turned up in the latrines. The results have shown that latrines are regularly placed along paths on the boundary of the territory. The bait to encourage badgers to swallow the plastic along with the food is molasses and peanuts. The method has been found to be quicker than using radios in showing the range of each badger colony, but radios are a fascinating day or night way of locating individuals and following their progress when on the move.

Cheeseman and Kruuk have found that the smallest badger territories in parts of Gloucestershire are about 40ha. (100 acres); a more typical area also in south-west England is about 70ha. (175 acres), and in low-density areas in Scotland about 180ha. (400 acres). The smallest recorded territory in Gloucestershire was 15ha. (37·5 acres) and the largest in Scotland was 309ha. (772·5 acres). Remember that each territory may include between 2 and 15 badgers or more.

The home range is that part of the territory most regularly used by badgers over a certain period: in the case of some sows in spring in quite large territories this can be only 12ha. (30 acres). Certain sows will also defend the immediate area around the sett entrances where they have had their cubs.

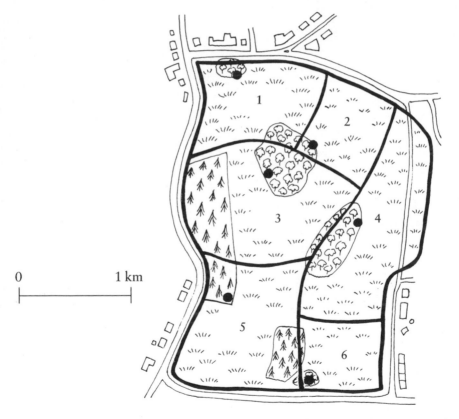

Sketch map of six badger territories to show how their size will vary according to availability of food: those with large pasture areas and numerous worms need less space; those with conifer plantations which lack worms will need access to other habitats. Main setts are also shown.

The size of the colony and its territory depend on available food. A daily need of about 200 earthworms can be taken in 2 hours on a still, wet night. Most worms are about 5 gm in weight and badgers feed nose to the ground, locate each one, pick them up delicately with the teeth and swallow them unchewed. Worming is easiest in short grass, but newly ploughed and harrowed ground may also make worms readily available for a time and woodlands provide excellent moist, sheltered feeding grounds amongst the shorter ground flora. Woods which only have 3 – 4 worms per square metre compared with 9 in pasture would still be very valuable due to the shelter from the wind, which worms hate.

Kruuk has concluded that if a single badger had the variety of habitats it needed to feed itself in a single territory, these would have such long boundary strips it would be impossible to successfully defend and also find time to feed during the hours of darkness. The very behaviour of the prey itself, by being available in one place one night, but not the next, forces their predators into groups.

The colony I watch each night come to feed together, sometimes in a group of eight badgers, but their behaviour to each other shows all the vital features of how large carnivores can live together in a territory successfully. The adult lowest in the pecking order appears to be a male who feeds nervously and rarely, if ever, receives appeasing scent marks (when one badger presses its gland under the tail against another badger). The dominant boar ('Capone') has the pick of the food and when he snaps or pushes the dominant sow ('Tufty') away from some delicacy, she does not rush off or challenge him. He growled at one boar as it approached to feed and made it cringe; he circled the new arrival, fed briefly and then lifted his tail and actually musked

against the boar's face before strutting off. Kruuk points out that this assertion of dominance without driving the other badger away saves the energy that would be needed to fight and all group behaviour has evolved to maintain peaceful group existence within the territory. The scent of the dominant boar will be marked on most of the other badgers so that the entire colony smells much the same, like a human family which uses the same brand of deodorant. I find the 'barging' behaviour of badgers, when they push with their ample flanks against each other, like a rugby scrum, in a dispute over food, very funny to watch especially when the boar lies down to feed in the ultimate demonstration of superiority. If the sow tries to push in, he will circle, sprawled across the food, to keep her away, then, suddenly, get up and walk away to let her feed as if it was of no interest to him. The dominant sow often gives old or young sows a hard time and 'Old Girl', the oldest sow in the group I watch, is not only frequently bitten during parts of the spring and autumn, but had to leave the main sett to have her cubs in an annexe sett before they were old enough to return to live in the central group of holes. Kruuk has found the sows do most of the digging although all in the territory share in this activity, as with the gathering of bedding, which must be dry before it is stored below ground.

The territory does, therefore, exist to ensure the survival of the colony and its strict maintenance explains many of the complex family relationships and behaviour patterns of badgers.

Regular artificial food in the same place each night results in relaxed feeding where adults sit and even lie down to eat.

Latrines and dung pits

An important feature of badger social life is the latrine, where dung and urine may be left over quite a wide area – several square metres in some cases. Within this you find small pits where badgers have dug out soil and turned to leave their faeces. Sometimes droppings are left without excavations and I often find single droppings around the orchard where I study badgers, with no attempt to dig a pit. Latrines in this area are built near the setts and this may indicate a less intensive territorial attitude when compared with the high density of Kruuk's and Cheeseman's typical boundary latrines (see p.63).

Sometimes several dung pits merge and appear to be covered up, but usually the dung is left exposed. Musk points are left where scent indicates the territorial ownership of the latrine. There will be signs of brown grass, caused by urine, which has an acidic content. Latrines have been invaluable in plotting territories and this has been well demonstrated by Kruuk and Cheeseman in their study areas in Scotland and England.

As well as studies using plastic markers (see p.63), Kruuk has also used harmless injections of radio-active isotope zinc 65 on one badger in each social group to estimate population size. By taking a geiger counter to the latrines over a two-month period he can pick out which droppings were left by that individual. If an average of only 1 out of 9 droppings react, for instance, this would give a population of 9 badgers present in the territory. Underground latrines have been found in excavated setts and are used when

(Left) *Soft badger dung in excavated pit after meal of earthworms.*
(Right) *Jelly-like autumn droppings after consumption of yew berries and plums.*

the badgers stay below in periods of very low temperature (see 'fossil dung', p.52).

I have come across one badger latrine which had fox and muntjac deer droppings close by. It was a secluded open clearing in thickets close to fields and must have been a very important if not to say powerful area of scent for the larger mammals passing through to the field edge. The latrines I have checked regularly in the wood surrounding our setts over the years appear to move about and vary in popularity but the same general areas are returned to time after time. Areas of deep loam under young hazels and elder have been regularly popular where a small sub-canopy exists under the mature trees. Field latrines may be close to fence posts, but others have no clear association with structures.

Although dung pits are relatively obvious, in recent research the clever use of dye to colour urine has been used (under licence, of course) to also show where badgers relieve themselves. Paddy Sleeman has sent me an advanced copy of a paper to appear in the *Irish Naturalist's Journal* jointly written with J. N. Cronin of the Zoology Department and P. Jones of the Department of Plant Science, University College, Cork which links the attraction of blow flies to stinkhorn fungi and badger setts. Paddy spoke to me about this on the telephone before I read the paper and I immediately thought of our main local sett and recalled the summer feature of stinkhorn fungi in the same corner of woodland. The connection is thought to be with carcases rather than urine and the paper also refers to Dr Neal's report of the use of the smell of stinkhorn to mask the smell of observers watching badgers. Sceptical scientists may raise a stink about this theory, but it would be worth investigating in woodlands near you.

A social group

One social group I have got to know well is illustrated. Relationships at a sett are always subject to change: due to deaths (such as road casualties); the arrival of badgers whose social groups have died out; or the departure of individuals due to aggression. Unsettled periods occur in March – April and August – September, but prolonged droughts may force badgers to exceptional movements caused by stress so that radical changes may occur in the identity of the colony.

The arrows indicate facial differences between eight adults used to tell them apart in a social group: (left to right, top to bottom) Curly ♀, Capone ♂, Twizzle ♀, Tufty ♀, Stripey ♂, Old Girl ♀, Goyter ♂, Quizzle ♀.

In 1986 there were 8 adults and 5 cubs in our colony. Capone was dominant and the suggested pecking order for sows over other females and boars over the other males is shown overleaf with highest at the top. Goyter looked very harrassed over winter 1986 and may have been on the verge of leaving the group. Old Girl, the oldest resident of the sett, whom I had seen since 1975, was badly bitten over winter and had her cubs in an annexe sett before returning to the main sett in May. Tufty, the dominant sow, appeared to be the cause of the injury and Old Girl may have also experienced loss of cubs to her in the past: hence the temporary separate nursery this year when

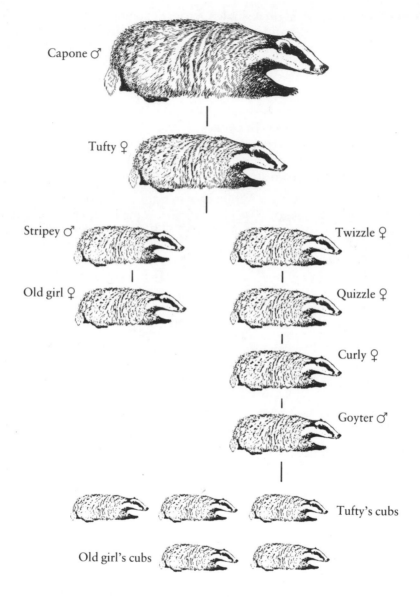

Capone ♂

Tufty ♀

Stripey ♂ — Twizzle ♀

Old girl ♀ — Quizzle ♀

Curly ♀

Goyter ♂

Tufty's cubs

Old girl's cubs

Pecking order of a known colony in July 1986. Goyter always looked rather scruffy and persecuted.

her cubs were born.

The notes below, taken on a single October evening, show how a colony arrives at the feeding area and indicates the time scale of watching during the evening. The main sett is about 400 m (440 yards) away. October is a time of much feeding and weight gain and the colony eats in a very relaxed way together.

October 3rd, 1986
Feeding in top orchard under Bramleys
20.25 hrs   First badgers arrive. 2 of Tufty's 3 cubs up, Harpo and Groucho. Harpo has distinct black edge left ear. Groucho has pink lump over right eye and has lost black hair from stripe.

20.37 hrs   3rd cub up: Chico. White spot in right ear like Harpo: ticks? No sign of Old Girl's 2 cubs for 2 weeks. She has come back since the August disappearance.

20.44 hrs   Stripey (♂) up, Groucho wanders off.

20.50 hrs   Stripey has gone, Twizzle (♂) arrives, Harpo still feeding.

21.00 hrs   Stripey back, feeds with Twizzle, Harpo trots off.

21.03 hrs   Old Girl (♀) arrives. She is huge.

21.06 hrs   Quizzle (♀) arrives: 4 badgers feed close to each other. Dogs barking—badgers look up, then resume feeding. Old Girl has not such a pale shoulder after the 1986 moult and the scar over her tail from the fights of last year does not show up any more. Her cheeks are as wide as any boar: old age has given her a very solid look.

21.16 hrs   Car disturbs all. Fox barking. Not seen one here for a few days, but one was sunbathing on cordon edge yesterday, 100 m away.

21.25 hrs   Quizzle arrives, but car disturbs again.

22.15 hrs   Twizzle back alone.

22.30 hrs   Capone (♂) up. He is dominant boar and has a mild shoving match with Twizzle.

22.32 hrs   Tufty (♀) makes first appearance, eats with Capone. Her cubs seem very independent of her now.

24.15 hrs   Heavy rain. Capone still feeding. Goyter (♂), the lowest in pecking order, up. Cautious near Capone, who ignores him.
I am going to bed now.

January Sows pregnant. Activity irregular.	February Peak of cub births. Courtship noisy.	March Peak of road deaths. Much bedding collection.	April Cubs explore to sett entrance and may emerge.
May Frequent mating. Cubs explore around sett.	June Sows cease lactation by end of month. Early evening emergence.	July Cubs 6 kg (13lb) feeding themselves. Droughts may increase road deaths.	August Frequent digging. Cereals taken in droughts.
September Movement and much bedding collection as well as digging.	October Fruits in diet. Rapid weight gain.	November Emerge late.Least mating activity.	December Sleep longer and deeper. Implantation of eggs in sows.

The badger year.

Watching nearly every evening and making notes produces an interesting pattern of behaviour. Although with binoculars you get to know the identification marks of individuals, early notes remind you of how long you took to be confident of 'who's who at the zoo'. Points from a year 1986:

January Inactive or rare visits December 28th – January 21st. Temp – 4°C to – 10°C most of this time. One lethargic badger 19.00 hrs on 12th, 2 up mild misty night 22nd. 29th Capone up and Old Girl flattens to him. She is badly scarred over tail.

February Very cold. Erratic visits. One badger killed when run over 1 km up road, but not from our social group. Capone, dominant boar, has fight scars and Stripey, a lower order boar, too. Neck chew marks on Tufty 24th indicate mating (– 4°C). By 26th normal feeding established, with pairing up obvious.

March At first feeding in more isolated way, not like autumn groups.

Lactating sows look hungry by 4th: it has been exceptionally frosty into this month. Foxes feed close to badgers. Feeding in snow 7th, 20.58 hrs. Back to group feeding; Old Girl has cubs in annexe sett. Fed for 45 minutes, face still covered in red sand from digging out sett. Old Girl fed early and most throughout March (found later she was lactating). Gales make them nervous. Old Girl's scars healing.

April   Fox, badgers and muntjac feeding together 21.42 hrs on 16th. Fox keeps distance. Tufty also lactating. Regular social feeding.

May   Lactating sows look very heavy in milk. Cubs seen around sett, but not seen in feeding area yet. Social feeding.

June   Cubs regularly seen feeding with sows after 4th: Old Girl has 2, Tufty 3. Cubs seen to flatten to Old Girl when approached, musked and left with her. Fox and cubs feeding with badgers and cubs. Fox cub greeted vixen with tail wagging and flattened ears 18th. 4-month-old badger cub fluffed up and growled at fox, which retreated, 22nd. 3 fox cubs with badgers 26th, 21.45-24.45 hrs.

July   Push fights between sows, but social feeding. Cubs very large.

August   Stripey ($\male$) has fresh fight scar on crown of head on 9th. Thunderstorms make badgers very nervous. Old Girl disappears with cubs. Not all adults seen. Wet summer.

September   Back to normal groups again. Old Girl returns, but her cubs not feeding with colony. More pairing up again. Capone musked on Stripey's head on 26th. Voracious feeding and large groups.

October   Large feeding social groups much of month. All very heavy and well fed.

November   Social group feeding. Still feed in pairs.

December   After 7th little interest in feeding, erratic. 2 sows which had cubs in the following spring both seen feeding 03.20 hrs 16th and 22.45 on 21st. Not seen or very rare visits from 28th.

Breeding and delayed implantation

Badgers can mate in every month of the year, but particularly from February onwards, as soon as the litter (or litters) of cubs are born in the social group. If food conditions over the whole period of growth are very favourable, a female cub can be successfully fertilized in her first autumn and have cubs around her first birthday.

There has been a lot of confusion about the mating behaviour of badgers, and Ernest Neal's painstaking field observations and research since his first work in 1948 illustrate this. The reason is largely because of the amazing reproductive technique of delayed implantation whereby the sow badger can mate at any time after her cubs are born, but still keep her birth time to the spring. In breeding colonies it is usual to observe a post-parturient oestrus which usually occurs shortly after the cubs are born; the sow or sows then become attractive and receptive to the boars. Badger-watching in February can be very rewarding because of the excitement of the boars whickering and purring after the sows which have become alluring again after pregnancy.

What does 'delayed implantation' mean? Both sows with cubs and those having their first oestrus will be able to mate and keep fertilized eggs, or blastocysts, unattached in the uterus in a state of suspended development.

Boar may chew at neck hair during copulation.

'. . . and when we go out tonight don't get fresh in front of that badger watcher like you did last time!'

They live off a minimum of food and oxygen from the uterine wall until they implant in the actual tissue and begin to develop as foetuses around the end of December. Ernest Neal made a particular study of reproduction and has shown that further oestrus cycles and mating can occur despite the presence of blastocysts in the uterus. This makes for a highly successful breeding rate and explains the confusion caused to some early naturalists who could not understand how an animal taken into captivity one spring and left alone still produced cubs a year later. Delayed implantation, which is typical of other members of the weasel tribe too, allows the species the maximum opportunities for mating and at the same time ensures that cubs are born at the best time for healthy growth. Conditions will vary from year to year, but they are suckled in what can be the difficult period, weaned when food is plentiful (in May usually, except in a dry summer when many cubs die) and should be well grown by the autumn, when fat is built up before the privations of winter. If you feed badgers as I do, you will see in December when the nights are longest that emergence generally becomes very unpredictable and erratic as if the badgers in a colony have lost their enthusiasm for food after gorging themselves through the autumn. December badgers also look very fat and one advantage of rapid growth by cubs due to regular food put out for them is that more will be capable of reproduction in their first year: the rapid growth of an artificially fed colony is due to several reasons, not just because there is always a staple diet available which prevents starvation. (Chris Cheeseman's work on the growth of cubs is frustrated at one sett in his study areas where a kindly householder puts out a marvellous diet of high protein food which produces exceptionally large cubs ahead of all the others.)

Modern research has not yet explained exactly what prompts the implantation of the blastocysts and so starts the cubs on their way to being born, but Ernest Neal points to the undisturbed, very inactive month of December in the sow's year as the critical time and there is growing evidence that disturbed setts produce fewer litters. So if you want your local badgers to do well, make sure nobody stamps around their setts, or shouts in the entrance in December (or at any other time, ideally). Ernest Neal suspects that the steroid hormones are taken up by the fat stored during summer and autumn and only become released into the bloodstream as the sow lives off the fat in her body during the dormant period. The secretion of steroid hormones cause the uterine lining to become receptive and so induce the implantation of the eggs. The stress of being captured led to one sow giving birth 15 months later: an amazing length of time for the eggs to stay alive before the sow's emotional state had stabilized enough for her to have her cubs. The cubs will be born two months after the blastocysts have implanted.

Apart from those fed by humans, colonies total little more than 12 with cubs, but in the highly favourable climate and habitats of S.W. England Chris Cheeseman has recorded one social group of 23 badgers where 3 lactating sows were present. This is the largest group recorded. It is, however, estimated that on average over half the cubs will die in the first year of their life and over a third die before they even emerge from the sett entrance. Although an equal number of males and females are born, twice as many males will die before they are one year old. The reasons for this are not yet fully known. When adult the boars tend to wander and explore further than sows and may be forced out of the social group by the dominant male. However, Ernest Neal found deaths of females were more common later in the year and a sample of road casualties gave almost equal male and female figures over the twelve months as a whole.

In very well populated regions the optimum breeding age is around five years of age for a sow and at this time 62% are having cubs. There seems to be a slow decline after this and if a sow does not breed, she has a higher survival chance. It must be remembered, however, that this information comes from Chris Cheeseman's high density study area in Gloucestershire and is probably not true in areas where badgers are relatively rare. In such circumstances sows would breed when young and continue throughout their lives (or until a social group built up). Chris Cheeseman suspected that badgers have a mechanism to regulate their own populations and his observations of female badgers in his study area with findings by other research workers would seem to confirm this. Copulation itself may

sometimes be brief, but long couplings of between ten minutes and over an hour are typical. (Anyone who has bred ferrets will know how some Mustelids can remain paired over several hours.)

However many badgers live in a sett, whether a pair or 15, certain patterns of behaviour are followed through the year. The dominant boar is very sexually active as the sows become receptive after the birth of the cubs (which number between 1 and 5, but most frequently 2) in February. January activity is irregular, particularly if freezing conditions extend over several weeks, but the spring movement of boars is marked and young males kept in a subordinate role in the main setts may seek sows in other territories. They risk attack from resident badgers and inevitably venture into habitats they are not very familiar with: many are run over on roads they may be crossing for the first time.

Underground the cubs are protected, fed and nursed by the sow in deep

Cub suckling from sow.

bedding collected carefully in previous months. How often adults kill cubs and how frequently setts are invaded by predators such as stoats, polecats or dogs which carry off young is unknown, but I remember how sad I was to see, as a boy, a two-week-old cub dead outside a sett. A year later I picked up a much older live cub which had been injured over the left ear. I had been watching this cub with its three litter mates for some time. The farmers who let me visit their sett (and called me 'badger boy') contacted their vet and the deep infected bite over the ear, as it proved to be, healed with injections of antibiotics. To get it used to the sett I would attach a lead and harness to the cub and walk it round the spoil heaps. It became very excited at the sett entrances and when we allowed it to return there was no further injury. Hopefully, in such circumstances, the dominant boar will accept the cub at once and set his musk on it as it arrives, so that it will once again smell like the rest of the social group.

The cubs that have survived the early weeks of musk-scented bedding, smooth tunnel walls and maternal warmth will emerge cautiously around late March and early April onto the mound of spoil outside the sett entrance. From being pink, blind and helpless at birth with thin coats of silver hair and faint black stripes on the face, they grow to be active, playful little badgers by the time they emerge so that the layout and scents of their home become firmly fixed in their senses. Their eyes open after five weeks – about halfway through this period – but they will never have the good distant eyesight of foxes, for example, and their noses will tell them most about the world in their life ahead.

Sows with cubs hurry back to feed them at night until, by early summer, they are out together. By June all juveniles will be familiar with the extent of their colony's territory: woods, fields and gardens, lake-side, cliff and moor, wherever they live. High summer will always be the critical time for food finding because the cubs are nearly as big as the adults and all will suffer if dry weather makes food scarce. They may search for food constantly from dusk to dawn. The autumn abundance of food in what is almost invariably a damp period fattens up the badgers and they become unpredictable in their feeding in December as the cold nights induce longer bouts of sleep, even torpor in some northerly countries.

Tragically people still enter terriers into setts, often choosing the very time when cubs will be with the sow to ensure that she will defend them and put up a strong fight. The sow spends much of her spring with the cubs and protects them fiercely. Each night she will return several times to the nursery chamber. The severe frozen weather in both February 1986 and February 1987, two of the coldest this century, made feeding on worms impossible for the sows rearing cubs, yet no reduction in litter sizes was noted in either year. Lactation must have continued largely from the diminishing winter store of fat and this would have drained the sow's reserves considerably.

The emergence of cubs outside the sett entrances at sunset in late April and May is one of the special delights of badger-watching. Regurgitation of food by the sow gradually weans the cubs onto solid items such as worms and beetles after three months, but an exceptionally dry spell may prolong suckling. Cub mortality during severe droughts is commonplace.

At setts with low badger populations I have recorded over several years the movement of families to annexe or subsidiary setts in summer, removed from the original breeding earths. As the colony grows, this movement is less obvious, especially if there are two or more litters in the sett at the same time and space is more at a premium. In large social groups one sow will move off to have her litter away from the main sett where the more dominant (not invariably older) sow may have her litter and may be aggressive. Male cubs are more likely to move to other areas or be forced away by fighting with old boars, but generally badgers stay in amazingly consistent social groups.

Cub development

When born cubs are only about 100 g (3½oz) in weight and little more than 12 cm (5 inches) long with 3–4 cm (1–1½inch) tails. In good conditions they are over 1 kg (2 lb) by 3 months, over 3 kg (6½lb) at 4 months, over 6 kg (13 lb) at 6 months and by their first birthday are over 9 kg (19½lb). This rapid growth rate comes from three months of the sow's milk taken during several feeds in each 24 hours as she lies in the bedding underground. A rich diet of worms regurgitated or carried to the cubs follows. They emerge from the tunnels before they are weaned.

Actual exploration accustoms them to locating their own invertebrate food in their fourth and fifth months of life. Over the years most badger-watchers will eventually come across the sad sight of stunted, under-sized cubs as well as the healthy ones. Very few of these will survive. On their first birthday, after twelve months of normal conditions, cubs will be about 75 cm (30 inches) long and their tails alone (at around 15 cm with hair) will be longer than their total body length when first born. Hair extends to several centimetres longer than the 12 cm (5 inch) length of the tail itself. They are tough, strong individuals and, even at eight months, well able to defend themselves and already contemptuous of foxes, for example.

 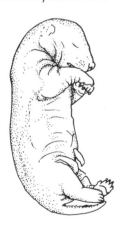 

(Left to right) *From three-week-old badger cub as a foetus to three days old as a cub with nearly full term foetus in centre (material via Dr Neal).*

Guy Fawkes

A lot of publicity surrounds November 5th to ensure that pets are kept indoors, but little thought is given to the effects of all the noise and lights flashing on wildlife at night. I have observed badgers on bonfire nights and they become very shy and nervous. Our local colony would not feed until the repeated bangs and coloured rockets ceased. Even late, when activities amongst the local humans had quietened down, they were highly disturbed and frightened if they emerged at all. When the 5th fell on a Wednesday I noted that the Saturday before and the Saturday after as well as the night itself were celebrated, each one causing the badgers to keep a low profile until after midnight. Away from human populations the effects are probably rather remote and less disturbing except in areas where there is a lot of night shooting on some farms from vehicles (of rabbits) which has a similar effect of scaring all and sundry at night. All of which leads me to suspect that the whole 1605 episode was just a cunning plot to ensure that badgers would be terrified around the start of winter for all time.

ALSO UNFAIR TO HEDGEHOGS HIBERNATING IN BONFIRES

'PENNY FOR THE BADGER

Do badgers hibernate?

As Prof. Joad might have said on BBC's Brain's Trust: 'It all depends on what you mean by hibernation.' Recent work in Scotland (Fowler and Racey) has confirmed long-standing opinions that our badgers have developed strategies to conserve their energy and body weight during the winter months when their normal diet of earthworms and other invertebrates are not available. Burrows used by American badgers in Wyoming were found to maintain a fairly uniform temperature between 1–3°C (Long). When the outside temperature was lower than −17°C the badgers stayed below ground. Both European and American species of badger are known to emerge from their earths on mild winter days. Two of the American species spent 70 consecutive days below ground and one radio-marked badger entered torpor on 30 occasions in this time. (Torpor was characterized by a more than 50% reduction in heart rate [55 to 25 beats per minute] and a 9°C reduction in temperature) [from 38°C to 29°C]. American badgers may therefore in latitudes with extreme conditions subsist all winter on their stored fat reserves. In Scotland Fowler and Racey also found that the body temperature was reduced from November to April so that mid-winter levels were as much as 8·9°C lower than in late spring. The lowest body

There is still much to be discovered about how badgers spend the winter underground.

On sunny, frosty mornings occupied sett entrances may steam from the badger's body heat below ground.

temperatures recorded were in December when the marked stay-at-home attitude of badgers is most influenced by daylight length and temperature. Their circadian activity cycles (biological processes that work on a 24-hour-clock) followed dawn and dusk most closely between January and May with particular peaks within two hours of midnight each day. The conclusion is that winter lethargy when body temperature is lowered by between 2 and 9°C allows great economy of energy and reduces the demand on fat reserves when there is little or no food available and temperatures are low. A pregnant sow was found to have three times the drop in temperature of non-breeding badgers and it is likely that this greater energy conservation ensures sufficient fat reserves for the demanding period of lactation after the birth of cubs around the end of January. Often snow or hard frosts will mean little food available just when the sow has several mouths to feed. There is, however, much work still to be done in this area, the research for which only involved a few badgers. We still do not have sufficient information to lay down hard and fast rules. So if your image of hibernation is a furry mammal curled up in a nest fast asleep from autumn to the following spring, badgers

do not hibernate. In fact, although their times of activity become much more difficult to predict in winter, badgers can still be very mobile and much depends upon the weather conditions. Our colony under surveillance in the winter months regularly feeds out in the orchard even in snow. Badgers in the extreme northern limits of their range may enter actual torpor and it is interesting that in Scandinavia there is an increased use of setts under houses the further north badgers have moved, probably as a result of the persecution of wolves (via my nephew, Paul Clark, [Sweden] and Paddy Sleeman, who gives a figure as high as 20% of setts under homes in north Norway).

Day out

You may think that badgers are nocturnal to avoid man, and this may in part be true, but their activity above ground is closely linked with the activities of their food. Earthworms and many other types of invertebrates such as beetles tend to be most active above ground in the hours of darkness. The times when the badgers emerge follow dusk with uncanny accuracy (especially January to April) and it is unusual to see them abroad in daylight. They do, however, emerge early in hot weather and I have known several occasions when activity in daytime has taken place in summer at local setts. Generally it is associated with more remote sites where there is less human disturbance and even outdoor nests are known. Disturbance can cause exceptional events such as the discovery of five newly born cubs in an open nest in hay reported by Ernest Neal in 1987. It was thought that the sow moved the cubs due to flooding of a nearby sett. Otherwise the presence of badgers above ground in odd human habitations such as outhouses, barns and cattle troughs has been associated with sick animals.

Atypical behaviour.

Hot underground chambers seem to make badgers emerge earlier, sometimes in late afternoon daylight, but it may also correspond with a very dry spell when badgers are hungry and eager to start feeding because they may have to hunt for food over wide tracts of land and still feel empty by dawn. One of the saddest sights I have seen of a young badger desperate for food occurred in the drought of 1976 when one was repeatedly spotted feeding out in a hay field in the afternoon. It was photographed for the local press and I did not realize at that time how easily food and water could have been put down to help it survive. It was pushing under cut hay as it dried and taking every insect it could find. It just ignored all people who approached. A week after I had watched the cub a friend reported that it had been found dead.

Badgers will emerge and re-enter their setts in the afternoon and cubs may play in a rarely visited woodland glade round a sett in daytime. I have often come across tree branches in sett entrances and always thought they were left there by interfering humans. Then one day I was by a sett when a branch partly underground gave a lurch into the hole. It was actually being pulled inside and for fun I gave a pull, too. After a few tugs the movement stopped and I found the branch had badger claw marks and hairs on the end. Tame badgers love to play with sticks and certainly chew wood, as anyone who has kept them behind doors finds to their cost. We have an old fallen oak by one sett which is used for play and is well rotted. It has now been chewed in two in one place as it has slowly disintegrated and much of the rest is in fragments where badgers have bitten at the soft bark to extract insects such as beetles or their larvae.

Bright lights are not, however, ideal for badgers and they tend to blink uncomfortably at sunlight or concentrated artificial light. The badger coat is not really suited to warm daylight hours and I cannot recall winter daylight emergence. The fact that there are underground dung pits shows how reluctant badgers are even to emerge at night in very cold spells. Snow, however, may raise the temperature at night in January or February and you often find tell-tale footprints to show that a trip out has been made.

In some remote areas badgers will on occasion sleep out in deep bedding in daytime, mid-summer to autumn.

Mutual grooming is common between badgers in a colony and individuals frequently set musk against each other.

A louse is located amongst the underfur in a badger's coat to be collected for identification in a jar along with a tick, a flea and other lice. An excellent review of parasites and infectious diseases of badgers by Martin Hancox covers the subject fully in Mammal Review 10:4, 151-162 (1980) *published by the Mammal Society.*

Why do badgers scratch?

If you take a road casualty badger into a warm room you will see why badgers are prone to a really good scratch when they emerge from their setts at dusk. Whilst the hair of their bodies may look immaculate from a distance, lice (Trichodectes melis) *will appear amongst the underfur as soon as you bring the body into the warmth. They survive the immediate death of their host but must miss the body heat and welcome a sudden change in temperature around them. You can see them clearly crawling about and it is best to keep dead badgers away* from the front room carpet. Fleas also trouble badgers, the most typical being Paraceras melis, *and it may be that these build up in such numbers in the summer bedding that badgers move from one sett to another as has been suggested in other carnivores such as brown hyenas. Three types of tick turn up regularly, those shared by dogs* (Ixodes canisuga), *sheep* (I. ricinus) *and hedgehogs* (I. hexagonus). One *road casualty I found had severe mange and numerous hedgehog ticks around its head, but this is very unusual.*

Causes of death

The most unpleasant scene of mankind's cruelty to badgers described to me by a friend was not of badger baiting, gruesome as such events must be, but of a sow which had died in a snare fixed to a path by her sett with the dead bodies of her three cubs. They had been forced by hunger to leave the earth to find her and died of starvation trying to suckle her. The sight of four decaying bodies lying against each other at a snare set by someone who could not even bother to visit it again for a week or more sums up how callous humans can be towards badgers. Historically, snaring, trapping, digging, and baiting have long been deliberate 'controls' (ways of killing them). In more recent times, shooting, gassing and poisoning have been common, but it is our motor vehicles which now take the greatest toll of badgers. In Idaho, USA, it has been estimated (Long) that 45% of the American badger population are killed annually on the roads. There are no figures for Britain, but there may be a similar percentage; just as there are areas where recent badger digging has made the species locally rare or absent.

Much could be done to make roads less destructive, but fencing and adaptations such as underpasses (see p.108) are expensive. Having protected the species by law (see p.113) we should now allocate funds to ensure its survival. We kill about 5,000 people annually on our roads in Britain and the USSR has published its own figures for the first time which indicate 30,000 people die on their roads annually. This may put into perspective how we tolerate an amazing rate of death and injury in our own species, let alone amongst the other animals we share the land with.

Railways also cause badger deaths especially when newly electrified at ground level. Things can be done to minimize the ill-effects for badgers: crossing places can be researched and the danger removed to ensure the safety of the animals. None of these controls on badger numbers has ever been quantified accurately. Bovine tuberculosis control is discussed elsewhere (see p.98) and for ten years drastically reduced numbers in parts of south-west England. The disease itself can be fatal to badgers, but not invariably, as can mange which occasionally occurs. Abroad rabies can be contracted by badgers and there are records of lungworm infestations. Otherwise they are robust mammals and only occasionally do you find a weak individual killed by roaming dogs or lethal bites from other badgers. This last type of mortality is an important aspect of social group behaviour and accounts for a proportion of badgers each year, usually when young.

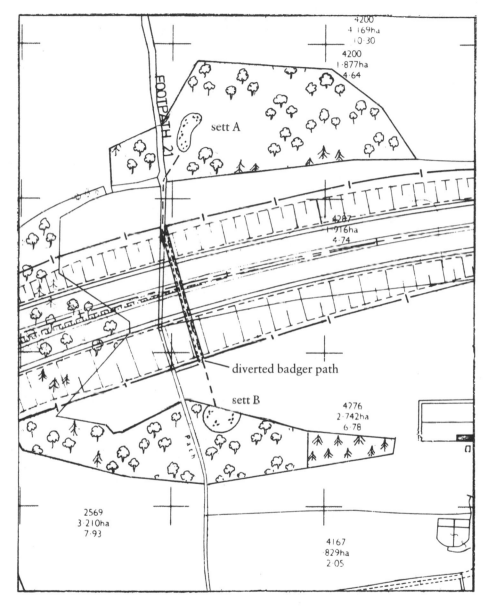

Detail of a motorway route map: new roads between setts result in badger deaths unless diversions are incorporated (see p.108). Badger-proof fencing lines the road on each side.

Badger funerals

The stories of badgers walling up their dead, dragging them back from road sides where they have been killed and similar events may have been observed, but the myth that they bury their dead has not been corroborated. Dead badgers left by their setts are usually ignored or receive little attention from other members of their social group. Accounts of sows taking dead cubs into the sett entrance conflict with the fairly frequent occurrence of dead cubs being found left abandoned outside holes or near setts and may simply indicate that the sow is still treating the juvenile as a living member of her litter. Many species of mammal will remain with and defend young long after they have died, but this is more common when there are single offspring rather than a litter.

The idea of burial may have arisen from the frequency of bones being found amongst the excavated soil on spoil heaps outside sett entrances. I recall it to have been more common in days of sett surveys when badgers and foxes were being gassed because all holes were treated just in case rabbits used them (often as part of the work of rabbit clearance societies). The technique was to cover holes with soil after a spoonful of Cymag crystals had been placed in the entrance or use pumps to send the gas round all the tunnels and chambers, blocking holes when white dust appeared. Any animals killed by inhaling the gas given off from the crystals in the damp tunnel air would die underground and their bones only be excavated when another badger, fox or rabbit reopened the entrance. The re-use of the sett may have been a matter of weeks, months or even years later. When soil and old bedding was dug out the bones would go with them, often buried in the spoils until rain or more digging revealed them to the passing badger sett recorder. Gosh! Evidence of an underground burial! Thankfully gassing of badgers is strictly illegal now, but setts are still likely to be the site where injured or sickly badgers stay or retreat into when approaching death. It is now known from Hans Kruuk's studies that badgers may kill cubs in their own social group and even dominant sows so injure subordinate sows that they die. He has also twice found very small cubs dead on latrines.

Badger-watching

My first attempts at seeing badgers were a dismal failure. I had found a sett near my home, went at dusk and kept downwind from the entrances, but had not planned my approach or waiting position. The badgers nervously slipped away out of sight. A farmer kindly let me try a sett on his land in the next village on condition I let him know how the animals were getting on. After a couple more unsuccessful nights I saw my first distant badger walk past in almost total darkness under the tree canopy on a path by the entrance to its huge underground home. I still remember how exciting that moment was. Generations of badgers had lived on this farm and their diggings had created mounds of soil outside the holes which now looked like part of the hillside itself. Because badgers are so well known today you can usually contact badger enthusiasts in local County Trusts or through the Mammal Society and badger groups who may be prepared to take you to see badgers. An experienced guide should increase your chances of success.

The most important thing is to get permission to watch before you do anything else. If you came across a sett by chance and decided to watch there you might barge into a site where another keen watcher was making a study of the badgers and upset them and the watcher, quite apart from the landowner, many of whom look after the badger setts on their land very carefully and may take you for an enemy of badgers. So find out who owns the land and call on them for permission to visit the sett.

If possible, first go to the sett with the landowner because he or she will

When walking at a distance from its sett, a badger which scents possible danger will trot off with head raised in an awkward, alert way. Noisy, high winds may also frighten them into this response.

often have stories and observations to tell during your conversation and may be able to give you tips on where the badgers move about the area. Try not to tread on the entrance soil at the sett itself as you check which holes are active – in fact the further you keep back, the better, because the occupants 'down under' are nervous, wild animals used to every kind of mistreatment by man. It is better not to disturb a sett in this way on the day you go to watch, but if you do, make sure your inspection is several hours before you watch. Some badgers are very tolerant and make a mockery of such advice but you won't know how nervous the colony is until you get to know them.

The more you watch, the better your chances of learning how the badgers live round their setts. Your visits are unlikely to become a routine and badger-watchers have a fund of 'disturbed courting couple', 'badger meets fox' and 'I heard this thunder of hooves and found thirty cows racing me to the field edge in the dark' stories.

The first rule of watching is *stay downwind*. Scent is by far the most disturbing thing to a badger and if the air has the slightest taint of human odour in it, the badgers will bolt or stay below ground.

Dark, warm, inconspicuous clothes are best, but I have known people in light clothing succeed. It really depends on whether you want the badgers to behave normally and not spot you. They may think your sky-blue jacket is an old fertilizer bag blown into the wood, but it is hardly conducive to relaxed behaviour. Badgers will stare and bob up and down at anything unusual but scentless, trying to make out by sight what the object is. They will snort and sniff at the air in suspicion and usually trot off.

The next most important aids to success are sitting still and making no noise. Resist the temptation to whisper to a companion and do take a cushion to sit on: comfortable watchers make the least movement. I am not of the 'enjoyment only comes through suffering' school of thought. Positioned downwind, in dark clothing (possibly with mask over face), sitting comfortably against a tree to hide your silhouette, you should be lucky and see the badgers, if they are active at the sett. Distance from the holes depends on terrain but start off no closer than about 10m and try to be above the entrances so that if the wind changes or gusts round the site, scent will still tend to rise up and away from those incredibly sensitive wet nostrils (the badger's, I mean). May and June are good months to start watching, but tough badger enthusiasts find February very rewarding because of courtship and vocal communication within the colony. Since badgers generally emerge at dusk, arrive an hour before then, earlier in mid-summer when cubs especially may emerge in the light. At dusk objects round the sett begin to look like the faces of badgers. These mirages keep the interest going until a face actually does appear, testing the air generally, before the badgers emerge fully. With luck the family may play and explore all round you for twenty minutes or so before individuals wander off to feed and enjoy the night's activities. Retreat unnoticed if possible.

'Dusk' is a good insect repellant, which seems more discreet and effective than others. Binoculars around 10 x 40 type will work well in poor light. Insects can be a real nuisance in July and August.

Is feeding badgers wrong?

If you are lucky enough to live close to badgers you may be tempted to put food out for them at dusk. Many people do now and it poses the question: can it harm the badgers?

I am guilty of the practice myself, but it all started by accident. My wife had a number of hand-reared deer which were released into the wild next to our garden. Because the deer were accustomed to dried dog food (Gilpa-Valu by Gilbertson & Page) we wanted to keep feeding them this until they were adapted to an exclusively natural diet. The deer returned to the food (one came back after a break of eight months, walked up to us and enjoyed a meal before leaving again) but in the meantime the local badgers had also discovered the tasty mixture of dry meat pellets, cereals and crushed dried peas. So we kept feeding them, provided drinking water close by, increased the lights from our house and finally attracted them to come under the bedroom window, illuminated by two 500-watt spotlights. This enabled the badgers to be studied in detail as they fed and allowed me to photograph and video-record their activities.

Our colony has grown from 3 or 4 some years (down to none 20 years ago when road deaths exceeded replacement by cubs) to over 15 now, partly due to the regular nightly food supplement. The diet is safe (water should always be available with dried animal foods) and in wet weather they often ignore it when they hurry away to the pastures to catch and eat earthworms by the dozen. It means that they go through the winter very well fed with ample fat reserves and the sows stay in peak condition when the cubs are feeding from them in the worst weather conditions.

Road casualties, extended freezing conditions in spring and prolonged drought may result in deaths of healthy badgers either as adults or as cubs. Although it is not true of every locality, where I live the ever-increasing road traffic exacts a relentless, indiscriminate toll on the badgers. So I have no regrets that the food we leave out is an artificial lure to help compensate for the loss of numbers. They only treat it as part of their diet: they ignore it when the rain brings out their natural, preferred menu of cordon bleu worms and they remain as shy of humans as any other wild population. The regular diet clearly increases the survival rate of the colony resulting in more cubs which might otherwise have died due to lack of milk in a hungry or under-nourished mother.

Other suitable habitats may be colonized and new territories established as badger numbers increase. It does not mean an ever-increasing population which will produce 'too many' badgers in one place causing predation on farmers' livestock or crops. Even the most suitable sett complex never seems to include more than about twenty badgers in one territory (see p. 67) due to the natural movements most frequent in August, September and March. So I am convinced tha feeding badgers does good, not harm to the local population, although colonies enclosed by urban development have been known to build up to abonormal numbers of thirty or more with artificial feeding where dispersal is no longer possible.

Badgers endear themselves to everyone who sees them from houses or hides, with or without illumination, as mysterious animals of the night. Dried pet food caused some problems with cats when it first appeared and owners did not make water freely available. There was talk of kidney damage in some species. However, badgers seem only to prosper on Gilpa 'Valu' and we have had one sow who still came to eat into old age, well beyond fifteen years, until she was sadly run over when the opening hours in our local public houses were extended. The later exodus of cars past where she lived caught her out and she was hit by a speeding motorist; this was witnessed by a cyclist following on behind who kindly brought her body in to show us. When feeding at the Gilpa mix she would lie down to eat like a citizen of Rome at an orgy, and was well built and sleek to the end.

She lives on as a mounted specimen in the schools' collection of the North Hertfordshire Museum Service loan scheme and Martin Hancox reported on her considerable age from the dentition when he examined her skull. As Martin said in the joint paper we produced on the 'Longevity of a Hertfordshire badger (*Meles meles)*' in the *Transactions of the Hertfordshire Natural History Society*, Vol 31: Part 3 May 1992, '...there is no further tooth eruption to replace worn or broken teeth, which sets a finite limit to longevity...it has hence been said that mammals "dig their graves with their teeth". The record longevity for the badger is a captive sow of 19.5 years old, but fewer than 10% of wild badgers attain the 10-15 year old age class characterised by *very marked* wear of the upper and lower molars, plus incisors...'

I am, therefore, all for badger 'tables' especially if they are helping old individuals to survive and keep all age groups healthy during droughts. It is, however, vital *not* to feed sweet things that will cause caries in teeth, or any meat which may cause food poisoning.

Badger damage

It would be difficult for a large carnivore (even one with a basic diet of earthworms for much of the year and which is relatively inactive in very cold weather) not to impinge at all on man's interests. We do, after all, want to have everything our own way. Common complaints I have received over the years are of damage to standing cereal crops, sweetcorn cobs, lawns and gardens. Badger setts may extend under drives and cause parts of gardens to fall in, usually because a house is constructed in a place where badgers have lived for years beforehand. Very rarely conditions result in extensive damage to golf courses and in south-west Hertfordshire parts of a fairway were dug up and rolled back like carpets by badgers who wanted to eat the cockchafer grubs and earthworms hidden below the top grass in a dry spring. As many as six badgers were seen working a section at a time. I found that the turf (which is in a woodland setting) was very thin and the roots shallow; pasture would not respond in the same way. In such extreme cases, the best answer

Ground under repair: extensive spring damage to both sides of a fairway at Ashridge Golf Course, Herts, where badgers dug out cockchafer grubs during a very dry spell —to the extent of rolling back the light woodland turf in places.

is to eliminate the food item so that there is no need for the damage. In places where soft fruit, such as strawberries, and sweetcorn are taken, electrified sheep mesh fences have been effective. The damage to cereal crops (oats especially) is only short-term, whilst the seed matures, but modern combine harvesters will lift up trodden corn and any seed eaten is much the same as that taken by flocks of birds. Badgers are best left alone; interference may induce greater problems, as is discussed in connection with stress and the incidence of TB (see following chapter; tension from aspects of life beyond the control of the individual are known to have an important part in events when a disease seems to be 'triggered' in that person. Capture of badgers and the disruption of social groups by control measures may produce the very distress that makes badgers susceptible to TB).

Badgers (and other mammals) should be fenced away from any possible prey items. They have been known to get into chicken runs and kill fowls and may take occasional eggs from ground-nesting birds, but they are quite different from foxes in their approach to food: live pheasant encountered by chance quickly fly up out of the way and are not chased. Rabbits are dug up as juveniles in the nest, not pursued and caught as by a fox. The small amount of crop loss from badgers must surely be outweighed by the benefits they bring – reducing rabbit litters every year as well as consuming insect pests, such as cockchafers. Kruuk shows how badgers will exploit 'patchy' supplies of food when such concentrations occur, such as at rabbit warrens and where sheep and deer carcasses frequently occur in hill or mountain areas.

Roger Symes has researched the nuisance value of badgers. Expense and delays were incurred when farm vehicles broke through into tunnels. Cattle were at risk in the same way in field setts where they could injure legs in a fall, and some crops such as oats, strawberries and grapes were eaten. These were the most common complaints, but the majority of farmers tolerated their badgers. Most West Country farmers he contacted felt that there had been an increase in the species since protection first came into force in 1973. In gardens anti-social behaviour includes tunnels in unwanted or dangerous places and dung pits dug into lawns. ADAS (the Agricultural Development and Advisory Service) and the badger groups have taken on a very helpful advisory role and will always attend to people with difficulties on their land, whether farm or garden. Of all the protections electric sheep fencing is best, but not invariably successful and at about £100 for a garden and £1,000 for a cereal field, there is a price to pay. Perhaps they could be shared round on a loan scheme as different types of crop ripen. The most expensive damage Roger Symes reported was to a road embankment which culminated in repairs and the construction of an underpass for the badgers to the tune of £25,000.

Badgers and TB

Having trodden a narrow path through the potential minefields of agriculture down the centuries, suddenly in 1971, badgers became the centre of attention in the farming world. In little more than a decade after a badger was found dead from bovine tuberculosis in south-west England, more than

Brief encounter: research has shown that badgers avoid direct physical contact with cattle and keep very much to themselves when feeding or crossing pasture.

10,000 badgers had been deliberately gassed as part of a control programme which cost over £10 million, yet the prevalence of the disease in cattle, which prompted the action, is little different today from its pre-1971 incidence.

One of the most frequent questions people ask of those making a study of badgers is: 'Do badgers really get TB and pass it to cattle?' The answer to the first part is simple: yes, they do suffer from tuberculosis in certain circumstances; the answer to the second part is more difficult: the evidence, despite all the work on the problem, is still circumstantial. Unfortunately the confusion in the public mind is due partly to the reluctance of the ministry responsible (the Ministry of Agriculture, Fisheries and Food, referred to henceforth as MAFF) to make public much of its deliberations, and partly to the media coverage, which we will discuss later.

I was asked in 1976 to serve as representative of the Mammal Society on the Consultative Panel set up by MAFF to monitor the actions taken soon after gassing operations commenced. I remained on the panel for eight years and was able to visit the centres of control and research as well as attend between three and four meetings each year in the MAFF committee rooms in London. To simplify what can be a long and confusing story I have made a summary of some relevant events in chronological order:

1882 Robert Koch identifies tuberculosis bacillus. Popularly known as 'consumption' it was estimated that 1 out of every 9 people born in the civilized world died of the disease.

1934 40% cows infected with TB in Britain (*Mycobacterium bovis*). Source of disease transmission to people in milk not pasteurized.

1935 1st voluntary national eradication programme starts.

1939–45 All work ceased due to Adolf (who could have been an even greater threat to badgers than MAFF).

1950 Compulsory eradication programme re-starts: areas considered 'attested' after all herds tested twice and all cattle which showed positive reaction to the test slaughtered (known as 'reactors').

1960 Badgers increasing generally, but regularly gassed with Cymag along with foxes and rabbits by farmers and keepers. Disease declined to negligible level: incidence of reactor herds of cattle only 1 in 50 by now.

1960–70 Incidence falls, apart from south-west England. (Slaughter policy had begun in Scotland and worked south.) Vets suggest wildlife be looked at as the cause of the disease. Badgers widespread and in south-west

'Ye gods! They're making beer out of us now!'

numerous. Widely snared and gassed unofficially although great increase in public interest in the species.

1971   Badger found dead from *M. bovis* in Gloucestershire.

1973   MAFF concluded badgers were a reservoir of infection and action was required where they posed a threat to cattle. Act to protect badgers was passed but it authorized MAFF to issue licences to kill badgers to prevent spread of disease. Lesions caused by TB found to affect lungs and urinary system of badgers most: bacteria easily spread through infected sputum (in bites and fights) and urine (onto grass in fields). Many more bacilli found in badger lesions than in cattle lesions. Great concern amongst badger enthusiasts.

1974   Trapping, shooting and snaring found to be too time-consuming and unpopular: gassing was preferred by MAFF and accepted by conservation and animal welfare organizations as better than snaring: the lesser of two evils.

1975   MAFF powers of control in 1973 Act modified in Conservation of Wild Creatures and Wild Plants Act of 1975: licences for gassing issued, but only through MAFF.
Gassing operations commenced: August. Consultative Panel of all interested bodies such as NFU, NCC, RSPCA, Mammal Society, RSPNC set up to review work: September.

1976   Agriculture Act 1976 allows entry to land for surveillance as well as control operations. Consultative Panel continues to meet several times per year.

1977   After NCC agreement, Badger Order made which defined 4 control areas with unrestricted licensed gassing in south-west England: 2 Cornwall, 1 Devon, 1 Avon, parts of Gloucestershire and Wiltshire. Outside these areas badger gassing still on voluntary agreement with owners of land.

1978   Much public alarm at deaths of badgers. Proof that disease can be communicated between badgers and cattle elusive. Mistrust by public of secrecy in Consultative Panel dealings.

1979   Lord Zuckerman asked to take objective review. Gassing suspended from September until report completed.

1980   Zuckerman report concluded that on scientific grounds badgers constituted a significant reservoir of bovine TB. Recommended control should start again. Gassing recommenced in October 1980. Report published: *Badgers, Cattle and Tuberculosis*. All 14 recommendations accepted by MAFF and one was that the use of Cymag, the hydrogen cyanide gas, be more fully researched.

1981   Experiments with badgers and gas at Porton Down continue.

1982   At Consultative Panel meeting in July Minister makes dramatic entry and announces that research showed badgers do not die quickly and humanely (like rabbits and foxes) when gassed at concentrations sometimes encountered during operational work. Gassing would no longer be used for control.

1983   Live trapping established as control method and favoured by Consultative Panel, for additional carcases thus made available for research work. More scientific study urged by Consultative Panel.

1984   Zuckerman's recommendation of another full review 3 years after his one was published taken up: Professor G. M. Dunnet, Mr D. M. Jones and Professor J. P. McInerney asked to review policy. Research begins to show no connection between badger density and incidence of TB, that badgers avoid close contact with cattle and that infected badgers may not all die at once, but live on and show signs of resistance.

Wildlife Link publish report: *Badgers, Cattle and Bovine Tuberculosis.* Argues that because the control of thousands of badgers has brought about no reduction in the prevalence of TB in cattle, MAFF should review policy, release minutes of panel meetings, encourage more research and identify zones of no-badger interference.

1986   Dunnet report shows that the total cost so far of eradication policy c. £11·3 million. Research costs amounted to c. £4·3 million. Estimated saving of compensation and associated costs by eradication policy: c. £1·6 million. The eradication policy would never 'break-even' in financial terms. Dunnet concludes that there is unchallengeable evidence that badgers constitute a potential wildlife reservoir of bovine tuberculosis for cattle, but badger control by gassing resulted in a net economic loss to the nation; he felt if people had been asked if the benefits would have been worth the nation spending over £7 million of public resources over seven years, most would have said 'no.'

1987 - 1994   Over the past seven years there has been increased research into the nature of the problem, but we seem to be almost back to where we started from as far as badger management is concerned. MAFF announced a new 5 year cull of badgers at the end of 1993 in what is seen to be a further attempt to control TB in cattle. Martin Hancox, who has served on the Consultative Panel during this time and has been the leading independent monitor of decisions and research on the subject, finds the decision 'unbelievable' since it involves a cull of only TB badgers detected by a test which is only 41% sensitive.

To check the health of the badgers, they are trapped in cages and subjected to a blood test. If the test proves to be positive the badger is killed, but if lactating sows have been caught up, the stress may cause their milk to dry up and the separation from their parent is very likely to leave the cubs to die underground anyway.

It is not even certain that released badgers are, in fact free from the disease because the test is, as we have seen, less accurate than tossing a coin. The Zuckerman report found the testing impractical back in 1980 and the 1986 Dunnet team described badger culls as ineffective, uneconomic and logically should cease. There is obviously strong pressure from somewhere to ignore the advice given from the expensive advisory teams set up by the Government and you wonder what the point is to having such bodies convened if their conclusions are not accepted.

Unbiased research continues to support the two report views. For example, Paddy Sleeman has published in a 1992 study of Wildlife Telemetry, a paper on the long-distance movements in an Irish badger population which recognizes that TB is endemic in badgers in Ireland and Britain and management strategies require knowledge of the movement of badgers. He concludes that the fewer the numbers of badgers there are, the more mobile individuals become so that localized badger culling to prevent TB, both by MAFF in Britain or ERAD (Eradication of Animal Diseases Board) in Ireland, could be counter-productive. The long distance movements found were not confined to badgers with TB, but the widespread existence of the disease in wild badgers in certain areas could be explained by such dispersal.

We *still* do not know how a badger may contract TB from cattle or how cattle might be infected from badgers, although judging from the way badgers search under cow dung for food and feed from urine-contaminated pasture on farms where there has been an outbreak of TB in the cattle, they seem more likely to be the victims of any exchange. Professor Stephen Harris and Drs Julian Brown and Piran White of Bristol University found that nearly a third of urinations by badgers were away from the latrines which cattle tend to avoid anyway when grazing, and were associated with boundaries to fields (*Proceedings of the Royal Society of London*, 253: 277-84).

They found that the more boundaries, the more badgers marked these sites and when they checked places where repeated TB breakdown control measures had taken place, these were, in the main, places with a greater diversity of features - more boundaries. This does, at first sight, seem strong evidence of transmission through urine from badgers to cattle, but the connection has yet to be proven.

After the Dunnet report the conclusion was reached that the complete eradication of the disease was impossible and the best way to deal with the situation was to limit the transmission to cattle. Useful points for cattle management in the report were to prevent access to badger setts and latrines and to stop sharing the same food source. Badgers are attracted to cereals and dairy nuts and badger-proof troughs were recommended. Badgers should also be kept away from food stored in buildings. Since the report, over 122,000 cattle have been found to have been infected with Bovine Spongiform Encephalopathy or BSE. The news of this 'Mad Cow Disease' almost eclipsed the media interest in TB in cattle and it is significant that in

Some modern aids to research: a study area badger has a collar fitted with transmitter and reflective beta light. Image intensifiers allow night viewing. Receiver and aerial allow individuals to be located and followed.

Somerset, where new TB breakdowns have been found, there have been 9,000 cases of BSE.

Martin Hancox has given the example of how cattle TB carriers are missed and become the real problem in bovine TB - at least 0.1% of cattle with tuberculosis do not react positively to the standard skin test used to detect the disease and there is often a 'spring flush' of TB in herds when released from the more stressful conditions of overwintering in barns or cattle yards (*The Ecologist*, Vol 23: 4, July 1993). A blood test for cattle would have the advantage of being repeatable the next day and it is already possible to carry this out.

He has pointed out that the 16 or so Somerset and Welsh farms which suffered cattle TB breakdowns after being clear for up to 40 years have now given TB to 3 out of every 4 badgers on these farms. All TB cattle may produce infectious cow pats containing bacilli which can live for up to a year, so that badgers foraging for worms or dung beetles under these pats stand a very high chance of catching the disease. They are, Martin points out, acting as a good 'miner's canary' indicator of the severity of a herd breakdown.

Any badger culls are also pointless whilst cattle still appear to be giving TB to badgers - cattle are assumed to contract the disease by respiratory means from infected urine, a far less direct risk of contact than the badgers experience when actually feeding amongst infected cattle dung.

Ireland has long had a much greater cattle TB problem (65,000 cases each year compared with about 800 in Britain). Many of the same arguments about its eradication centred round blaming badgers, as in the UK, but they are negotiating a £80 million EC grant to bring in more accurate blood testing and computerized tracing of stock, which will shorten herd restriction times whilst tests are carried out. The selling on of TB cattle was a major cause of the spread of the disease in the past. Vaccine has also been tested in Ireland because MAFF would not allow this research to take place in Britain and to 'solve' the cattle-TB problem, the government envisages spending £1 million annually on culling, £750,000 on research into the negligible risk of badgers infecting cattle and some £30,000 on the TB Panel.

What are the alternatives? If we see immunization as the best strategy, what are the practical problems of giving badgers vaccine? We have seen that the national survey in Britain indicates 30,000 setts would have to be treated. If the solution to all members of a badger social group receiving the treatment is to bait up the vaccine in a tasty package and roll it into every entrance of every sett (perhaps 150,000 doses) a great deal of field work will be needed as well as the immunization of all cattle.

Martin resigned from the MAFF Consultative Panel because he disagreed with many aspects of policy including the expenditure of £11 million on culling, the failure to achieve any reduction in cattle TB over 17 years and the capture of sows for testing which has already, by error, left cubs to starve. Britain's obligations under EC Directives to eradicate tuberculosis in cattle costs nearly £8 million a year on routine cattle testing. This is a rather cosmetic execise since there are only some 800 cases a year in Britain, compared to a similar number of BSE cases *a week*. There is virtually no risk to public health from bovine TB with milk pasteurization almost countrywide and rigorous abattoir inspection. All this expenditure, including the badger culls, is happening whilst clinical TB research in humans can only muster £10,000 a year, and child vaccination programmes are being cut widely when there is real risk of TB in urban and ethnic populations still in touch with endemic African / Asian TB areas.

Studying badgers

There is so much still to be learnt about badgers that you can help in many ways. (See next section for organizations to join.) Plotting the location of setts is an enjoyable field activity which helps in our knowledge of the distribution, population and threats to social groups. By watching whenever possible all the year round and making notes you can build up a valuable set of observations which may provide a pattern alone or when collated with other studies.

Particular interest is being taken in the biology of badgers on themes such as reproduction and winter torpor, but any observations can help build up our knowledge of the species as long as they are completely factual and accurate. Never adapt data to fit a particular theory you have.

Much more needs to be known about social organization and how colonies move around between setts through the year. More research, too, is needed on diverting badgers from our roads. You can join a neighbourhood watch on setts to protect them.

If you are inventive you may also come up with techniques to reduce the nuisances badgers sometimes cause farmers, gardeners and householders. Help in all these areas is much needed. Good badgering, in the best possible sense of the word!

During the research work in Gloucestershire badgers were found to have moved 25 kg (55lb) stones to get to hidden food.

Conservation measures

The first priority in badger management is to conserve their habitats; obviously, a badger without a place to dig a sett or somewhere to feed will not survive. Protection of habitats is one of the aims of wildlife trusts, so do support your local one. (To find it, ask at your local library.) Over-population of humans has been the greatest threat to the world's wildlife and even in areas that seem to stay much the same from year to year simple, everyday developments can gradually reduce the success of a species. For example, sand and chalk pits were commonly dug on our farms at suitable geological sites to obtain building materials or to lime the fields. This century most of these sites have become neglected and colonized by trees to give numerous, attractive scattered copses. Such sites are ideal for all kinds of

Adapted Armco stream culverts to which the badgers are diverted by fencing make the best road underpasses: a path is built on one side (left) and the wire netting is attached to a post-and-four-rail fence (right) along the road for as far as badgers penetrate. It should be turned in towards the badgers. Old established paths may need extra deep burial and a longer turn to prevent badgers digging underneath. Bait trails will introduce them to the new route. Pipes should be 600-mm diameter minimum, the bigger the better. Fencing: 50 m rolls of 1.5 m wide 100 mesh galvanized wire sheep netting fastened by heavy duty staples. The use of culverts has been taken up abroad: in Holland, for example, 51 badger tunnels now exist with c. 100 kilometres of wire fencing used. About 1,000 badgers are known to be killed on unfenced roads in south-west England alone each year.

wildlife, especially badgers, because of the steep banks and cover, surrounded by fields which provide food all the year round. Standing crops often add even greater isolation during the summer. All such pits should be protected – but often they are filled with rubbish such as discarded chemical drums, glass and old asbestos roofing, all harmful as well as ugly when dumped. The trees can so easily be grubbed out now and the pits filled in that often the only memory left is a sandy or white depression in the ploughed land visible perhaps twice a year. Wilderness on a farm, however small an area, is essential to badgers, whose needs are remarkably modest.

Protection from vehicles when crossing roads might be the second most important conservation measure, especially as more and more roads are constructed to by-pass villages or towns and extensions are made to the motorway system. The Department of the Environment has probably done more than any government department to contribute to badger survival by sanctioning and financing fencing to keep badgers off roads and in some cases divert them into underpasses below new roads. They are very approachable and will consider proposals as long as local groups survey the badger setts thoroughly, show on maps where their main paths run and where feeding areas are disturbed by new roads. Badgers may cause

'Damned cheek!'

motorists to swerve at speed so that separation of the two can be of benefit to man as well as badger.

At last public opinion seems to be questioning the endless road-building obsession which constantly fragments habitats and consumes vast areas of our limited countryside, quite apart from its long-term effects from exhaust emissions, carbon dioxide and noise. This may mean that the actual causes of overcrowded routes are tackled rather than constantly adding miles of tarmac to our land as if this will ever answer the problem. Under the financial constraints on all public spending, it is increasingly difficult to get proper consideration given to diverting wildlife off new routes. Badger groups should persist, however, and do all they can to ensure that measures are included in all planning stages and then carried out when the work by the contractors takes place.

Forestry fencing is less common now (away from the massive planting schemes in mountain areas where deer are present) with the greater use of individual tree guards, especially the plastic tube variety which allows light through to increase the temperature around the tree and stimulates growth. However, where protective fencing is put up 'badger gates' on paths prevent damage to the wire by allowing the badgers to push through whilst the lighter, destructive rabbits are kept out. The gates must be constructed on well used badger paths and the animals have to get used to them initially.

Management in towns is necessary where badgers live in gardens and inevitably come into contact with humans by accident or through their digging activities. They can easily fall into disused swimming pools and an escape route such as a plank should always be in place. The RSPCA and local trust will help advise on problems such as setts undermining drives or sheds. In Sweden they seem to be particularly partial to digging under houses. Road casualties are very high in all countries where badgers are widespread and the ideal answer for all wildlife would be to fence all sections of country roads with a history of repeated road deaths and sites in urban areas where badgers have caused annoyance or damage and divert animals. Diversions through stream or farm culverts would maintain the circulation of wildlife between areas of countryside. Management is the answer, not control.

Badgers in difficulty

You may find a badger has become accidentally trapped in a garden or garage as a result of foraging at night or pursuing some kind of prey. In daylight or in the presence of man when they feel cornered badgers will roll up to protect their heads from attack. I have been asked to help with the removal of badgers in these circumstances and you should always involve the local RSPCA officer. They have great experience in handling different animals and it is useful to have an expert at hand, especially with a restraining noose at the end of a pole to slip over the badger's head as you approach to pick it up. Never do this with hands even if you have the strongest gloves because the bite of a badger in these circumstances is severe. Obtain a black plastic dustbin and ease the edge of this under the badger's head, as it stiffens even more into the rolled-up defence position. If possible slip the noose over its head (these are held on long poles and can be released at a safe distance for hands, too). The dark cavity of the black plastic dustbin (preferably empty) is more attractive to the badger than the surroundings it has found itself in and with a little coaxing, it should roll inside (the noose can now be removed). Immediately stand the dustbin up and secure the lid really well through each handle with rope. Remove the badger in the bin, keeping it as cool as possible, to the nearest safe area where paths and setts are known and carefully take off the lid. It would be ideal to do this in darkness when the badger is most relaxed outdoors, but do not keep the animal in the dustbin any longer than necessary. When you take the lid off, first it will probably stay curled up as if asleep, but all of a sudden it will come alive and circle the area to get its bearings. It should then trot off purposefully towards its sett. I have put a young badger directly into a sett entrance where the holes were close to a garage in which it was found. It bolted apparently happily and much relieved down the tunnel. The danger of releasing the animal into an earth remote from where it was found is that you might put an individual into another social group, which will then attack it, and may even kill it. All you can do is find the nearest and most likely site for release. If you transfer a cornered badger to a cage make sure that it is made of very small, strong mesh so that the badger cannot get its jaws round the wire and damage its teeth. To secure the badger so that an injection can be given to subdue it, use a movable inner side to the cage which allows you to pull it against one side. This is easier than using a blowpipe. The aim of any badger rescue should be the rehabilitation of the animal at the earliest possible time.

Wild badgers may turn up in the oddest places. If cornered when lost, sick or injured, they usually curl up in their defensive position in daylight. Translocation is discussed on the opposite page.

If they escape or live partly wild they are liable to experience attacks by resident badgers to their rumps or much worse before they are able to survive as free wild animals once again. Remember that the least territorial months of the year are the last seven.

Badgers found still alive in snares should be covered in a coat or sack and the snare wire cut away, preferably with long-arm bolt cutters. It is a lot easier with two people and it is best to go for help and get wire cutters rather than attempt to do the job alone. Call the police and RSPCA on the way so that they can witness that the illegal act (of catching a badger in a snare without a licence) has taken place and can investigate who is responsible.

Sick, injured and orphan badgers are best left to the professionals. The first lines of help are the RSPCA and your local vets. Stefan Ormrod is the RSPCA's Chief Wildlife Officer and the society runs a Wildlife Field Unit at West Hatch, Taunton, Somerset. Badgers rehabilitated from the unit are being fitted with biodegradable radio collars to study what happens to them when they are released. There is a great danger with any badger that you will get badly bitten and tame ones can never be fully trusted. I have known so many people to receive deep wounds from pet badgers in all kinds of circumstances. Diet is difficult in juveniles and a complete loss of hair can occur two weeks after cubs have been given a cows' milk based preparation. Individual badgers vary and Eunice Overend has found that the earlier cubs are reared, the less likely it is that this allergic reaction will occur. Goats' milk is just as bad in this respect and we found lamb or sows' milk replacer powdered milk preparations (available from agricultural dealers who are often associated with livestock markets) are generally much better than bottled cows' milk. It is useful to have a foster mother dog to prompt urination and to clean up the faeces which thus stimulates feeding. Otherwise you must do this yourself with cotton wool and warm water. Fed every four hours a cub should prosper. Any baldness will be temporary and the cub will re-grow the hair completely in time. If you go against all the advice and rear a badger you may have a commitment for some 14 – 15 years with a powerful carnivore which becomes more possessive about you than the average dog. As well as the RSPCA Wildlife Unit, Les Stocker (Wildlife Hospitals Trust, 1 Pemberton Close, Aylesbury, Buckinghamshire HP21 7NY, Aylesbury 29860) will give advice and help from his considerable experience in this field. In Scotland there is a busy twenty-four hour wildlife rescue service: Hessilhead Wildlife Rescue Centre, Gateside, Beith, Ayrshire KA15 1HT (Beith 2415). I have greatly enjoyed being with tame badgers, but can only repeat the best advice: do not be tempted to take them on yourself.

Badgers in law

If you see a vehicle such as a van parked suspiciously near a badger sett o
people with terriers and digging equipment it is best to keep your distanc
and call the police as quickly as possible. Be observant and note vehicl
registration details - a careful description made at the time of the number
of people and dogs, with any features of particular note, is worth severa
recollections made later.

Do not persecute innocent people working ferrets, but those who worl
terriers legally and with the permission of the landowners involved invari
ably behave differently from those who take a criminal pleasure in causin;
suffering to animals. The general public can be very helpful in this respect
At one time it was the policy of organizers of surveys of badger setts, in
cluding the Badger Groups and Natural History Society recorders, to keej
the whereabouts of these sites strictly confidential. Unfortunately this coul
result in setts being interfered with or even destroyed when people livin;
close-by were unaware of what was happening.

A much more successful approach is to make the locations well know1 to local people so that many pairs of eyes are likely to spot trouble before it is too late. Most of the calls I have received about threats to setts have been originated by people other than badger group members and there have been three occasions when neighbours have made telephone calls about people with terriers they have seen parking and walking towards a sett complex where I monitor the badgers. I was able to apprehend one man working a lurcher with a terrier as a result of observant neighbours and fully support the shared information policy.

The police have a network of local Wildlife Officers who specialize in dealing with the increasing amount of legislation concerning the country-side. Steve Kourik is an Inspector in our Hertfordshire Constabulary and he is the Force Wildlife Liaison Officer. He chaired our Badger Group for many years and I have found similar examples of close involvement by individual officers in badger conservation in Groups elsewhere in the country. I am indebted to Steve for providing me with all the material on the legislation he and his colleagues have to use to interpret and enforce the law on a day to day basis. A full list of the books and papers Steve recommends is given at the end of this chapter. The nature of the work and the increase in legislation concerning all aspects of wildlife prompted the production of a *Wildlife Law* guide to cover all aspects, but he has made an additional summary of the Badgers Act on which the following material is based. (Steve also arrives with vanloads of police on training exercises at our local sett to show the field aspects of any case which may concern them and I can only imagine the reactions of any diggers caught harming the earths when fifteen or so police happen to walk into the wood.)

Baiting of any animal was made illegal under the 1911 Prevention of Cruelty to Animals Act, but legislation aimed specifically at badgers only came about, after considerable pressure from members of the public, in 1973 with the Badgers Act. There were subsequent amendments as loop-holes became obvious and the Badgers Act 1991, with the Badgers (Further Protection Act) 1991, culminated in the Protection of Badgers Act 1992 which at last gave protection to the setts where badgers lived as well as to the animals themselves. The principal offences are:

Unlawfully killing or taking It is an offence for a person to *wilfully* kill or injure or take any badger or attempt to do so. (Exceptions include unforeseen emergencies when, for example, there is no other way of preventing damage to livestock in an enclosure.) The 1992 Act places the onus upon defendants to prove that they were not attempting to kill, injure or take a badger.

Possession of dead badgers It is an offence for a person to possess or control a dead badger or part of a dead badger. (Exceptions include a badger found to have been killed in a road accident where it is lawful to take possession of the carcass. However, due to the trade in mounted specimens and skins, anyone in possession of such an item will be guilty of an offence unless they can show that the animal had not been killed in contravention of the Act).

Police Powers Anyone found committing an offence under Sections 1 to 10 of the Act (1994) may be asked for their name and address and be ordered to leave land by the occupier, owner or their servants or a police officer. Police officers have powers under the Act to stop and search any person they suspect of having committed any such offences. This power also extends to searching any vehicles associated with the activity. If anyone fails to give their name and address or quit the land, they then commit a further offence under Section 5 of the Act. There is no power to remove anyone forcibly from the land, although the owner of the property could remove someone as a trespasser.

Cruelty It is an offence for any person to cruelly ill-treat any badger. (The act of cruelty can take any form and does not just apply to digging or baiting.)

Badger tongs It is an offence for any person to use tongs against a badger. (This was drafted because badgers react so violently to being restrained that people who catch them may use long handled tongs — see page 35 of this book).

Badger digging It is an offence for any person to dig for any badger. (The onus is now on the accused to show that they were not digging for a badger - the Act states that in any proceedings for an offence where evidence could reasonably be concluded to show that the accused was digging for a badger, they shall be presumed to have been doing so unless the contrary can be shown).

Killing badgers by prohibited means Even under licence it is an offence for any person to kill or take any badger by use of any firearm other than a shot gun over 20 bore or a rifle which uses bullets over 38 grams in weight.

Interfering with a badger sett It is an offence for any person to interfere with a badger sett by
(a) in any way damaging a sett or a part thereof;
(b) destroying a sett;
(c) the obstruction of the access to any entrance to the sett;
(d) causing a dog to enter the sett;
(e) disturbing a badger when it is occupying a sett *and* by intending to do any of these things *or* by being reckless as to whether their actions would have any of these consequences. A person would not be guilty of committing this offence if they were able to show that their actions were necessary

to prevent *serious* damage to land, crops, poultry or any other form of property. However, this defence can only be used if the action was required *immediately* to stop the *serious* damage. Otherwise the person must apply for a licence to carry out the action.

In addition, the activities of fox hunts are now covered in that a person would not be guilty of disturbing a sett by damaging it or part of it, or by obstructing access to any entrance or disturbing a badger occupying a sett if their actions were incidental to a lawful operation which could not have *reasonably* been avoided. This exception includes hunting with hounds *provided* that the person takes no action other than obstructing the sett entrances. This obstruction can only be done by the use of:

(a) untainted straw or hay, or leaf litter, or bracken, or loose soil placed in the entrances to setts **on the day of the hunt, or after midday of the preceding day or**

(b) a bundle of sticks or faggots, or paper sacks either empty or filled with untainted straw, or hay or leaf litter, or bracken, or loose soil, that has been placed in the entrances **on the day of the hunt and then removed on the same day.** The person who undertakes earth stopping in this way must have the authority of the landowner or the occupier and be authorized by a Hunt recognized by the Masters of Fox Hounds Association, the Association of Masters of Harriers and Beagles, or the Central Committee of Fell Packs. The Hunts *must* keep a register of all authorized persons.

Possession of live badgers

It is an offence for anyone to sell or offer for sale or possess or control a live badger. (Badger baiters often sell badgers to one another or keep the animal for some time prior to the badger baiting event. It would not be unlawful for a person to possess a live badger if they did so in order for it to be taken for veterinary treatment. Nor would an offence have been committed by someone who was transporting a badger which had been caught under licence. This is sometimes necessary when a sett is going to be destroyed through road or other development).

Marking or ringing live badger It is an offence for any person **not authorized by licence** to mark or attach a ring / tag / other device to any badger. (Researchers are often granted licences so that they can mark badgers for purposes of study, so it is permissible for a badger to trail out a ball of golden string behind it, Theseus-like, if scientists desire to plot their movements in this way and have the legal right so to do).

Orders for the destruction or custody of dogs Under the 1994 legislation, where a dog has been used or was present at the commission of an offence under the appropriate Sections of the Badgers Act 1973 (taking, injuring or killing badgers and offences of cruelty) the court, on convicting the offender, may, in addition to or as a substitution for any other punishment make either or both of the two orders

(a) an order for the destruction or other disposal of the dog

(b) an order disqualifying the offender, for such period as is felt fit, for having custody of a dog. The court may appoint a person to undertake the destruction or disposal of the dog and order the offender to pay expenses for its destruction or disposal.

Definition of a badger sett A 'badger sett' means any structure or place which displays signs of indicating *current* use by a badger.

Badger diggers

Anyone who takes pleasure in breeding and training terriers, which are large, sensitive and intelligent carnivores to attack other large, sensitive and intelligent carnivores (badgers) must – you would think – have a personality disorder. It is a mistake, however, to think that badger diggers set out at a given point in their lives and say, 'From today I will be a badger digger.' Phil Drabble in his book *Badger at My Window* describes how the use of terriers against badgers is very much part of the tradition of breeding, owning and working terriers. Although he was writing of a period before badgers were protected, attitudes die hard, especially in the hunting world, and badger digging is inextricably linked with fox hunting. Drabble found in the 1950s that the hunt terrier men would go round their known artificial earths at the end of the season and make sure there were no badgers present. If there were, these would be dug out and killed to leave the space vacant for vixens to rear cubs.

He describes the typical terrier man as living an almost gipsy life, breeding, training and selling terriers. He was on a retainer paid by the hunt so that should a hunted fox go to earth, he would be on hand with terrier and spade to flush out the fox which would then run on for the hounds to follow once again.

A badger designed by a committee? The dachshund or badger-dog (dachs=badger in German) known as a breed for more than 200 years in Germany and Austria. Nicknamed 'sausage dog' because of the distinctive shape which was intended to give easy access to sett tunnels in pursuit of badgers. At least twelve varieties bred including smooth (oldest), long-haired and miniature types.

Drabble describes earth stopping which was also the terrier man's job, but not so popular: it involved going out the night before each hunt and filling up potential holes into which foxes could escape. This meant the fox was less likely to need to be flushed from an earth so there would be no tips from the huntsman. He disliked badgers because they would demand a long dig to

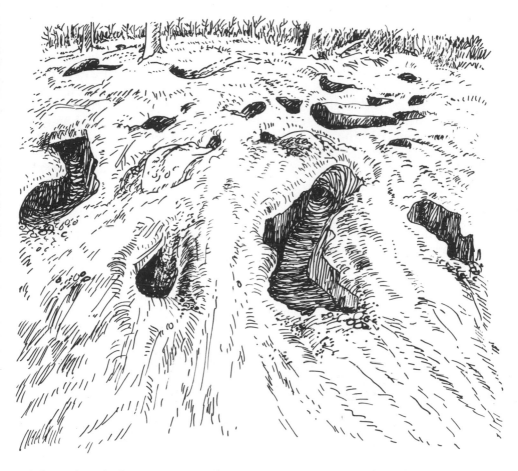

A flourishing badger sett is turned into a scene reminiscent of World War I trench warfare by men, spades, pickaxes and terriers. For this massive ecological damage, diggers, if caught, are often fined less than their quarterly central heating bill. In some parts of Britain monitored by badger groups c. 50% of setts are annually interfered with. In 1986 there were twenty-six prosecutions, twenty-four of which were successful.

extricate the terrier and kill the badger. Each hunt still has at least one terrier man and earth stopper.

Badger digging is, therefore, part of a whole world of owning terriers and working them against foxes, rabbits and rats, or sharing duties with long dogs, such as lurchers, for taking hares and deer. Baiting a badger may take place during a dig, or when one is cornered; young terriers as well as experienced ones are set onto the badger which may be restrained or injured in some way to give the dogs every chance of learning to hate the species without being killed. Alternatively, badgers may be put into a sack alive and taken to a pre-arranged location to be set on by a whole series of terriers in a secret pit.

The people who enjoy this sort of activity, whatever we think about their mental condition, are often associated with others in related illegal activities involving animals such as dog fighting, cock fighting and the importation of protected birds. In this world there is all the illogical camaraderie of criminals – the 'them and us' attitude to those who oppose such practices, the police and RSPCA officers.

The final control on these illegal activities will come when digging for foxes is also made illegal except under Nature Conservancy licence and the offences of either badger digging or fox digging without licence made to carry the maximum £2,000 fine, automatic destruction of terriers and confiscation of all equipment involved *including* vehicles.

No terrier bred for digging will be safe after it has been used in this way because even in the most loving new family it is likely to go straight to earth when taken on the first walk near setts or fox holes. The various types of Jack

Bitch smooth-haired Jack Russell—the most popular terrier for badger digging— which comes in a variety of coats, shapes and sizes. Dog bull terrier: the traditional baiting dog. In recent years North American bred pit bull terriers have been imported and some involved in dog fighting cases as well as badger digging.

Russell are the favourite type for badgers but I have bred these plucky terriers which daily pass setts and never go to earth simply because they are trained not to. Terriers can be as happy scenting after rabbits, rats and mice. They do not need to harass or kill large carnivores to prove their breeding or skill.

On one occasion I was called to dig a Jack Russell terrier out from underneath a shed where a badger had taken up residence. The dog had not managed to reach the badger, but throughout the excavations, which I had to do with a pickaxe through concrete to retrieve the dog, the unhappy badger was giving deep threatening growls. I located the position of each by the enthusiastic yelps of the terrier attempting to crawl up a narrow side burrow and the deep rumbles of anger from the badger.

Photographing badgers

The simplest set-up, which gives excellent results, is a tripod behind which you sit, leaning against a suitable backdrop to conceal your shape. Wear drab colours and camouflage any bright metal photographic items as much as possible. Use a tripod which has dual flash holders and have an adaptor which fires two flashguns from the camera contact or hot shoe. The choice of lens depends on local conditions and the distance you are from the badger sett: a 50 mm or zoom lens (such as 35–70 mm or 70–210 mm) should be composed and focused before the light fades. Ideally, use an autofocus lens and dedicated rapid fire flashguns which have an infra-red auxiliary light to activate automatically in dim light so that the lens will autofocus even in total darkness. All these are now available in the popular 35 mm camera ranges and I use the Canon EOS (Electronic Optical System) series and their very quiet Speedlite 420EZ flashguns. With the three frames per second motordrive you can try for a sequence of pictures of badgers, for example, playing, running or gathering bedding, as long as the flashguns are set on the low power setting which enables them to recycle very fast. Take your picture or pictures and slip away quietly when the badgers are out of sight. Do remember that repeated flash photographs every time a badger emerges will seriously disturb the animal and all photography should cease in dry spells when badgers need the whole night to get enough food to survive.

You can write endlessly about wildlife photography, but it all boils down to personal experience and what type of equipment you can afford. The very simple automatic cameras with one flashgun in the hot shoe may produce good results if you can get close to the badgers, but you get unpleasant 'red-eye' effects, and, if the badger looks at the camera, instead of eyes or

The amazing effects of rapid fire flash with motordrive . . .

even red-rimmed eyes you get two orange reflections glaring back at you in the picture. Flash indoors bounces off walls and ceilings, but outdoors it seems to vanish very quickly into the trees or grass because there is nothing to reflect the light onto your subject. You do, therefore, need at least two powerful flashguns off the camera: a guide number that gives you a 60th of a second at f 11 indoors may equal a 60th of a second at f 5.6 in the field. Recent developments in camera technology are amazing and have reduced problems of photography in the field – weak flash contacts which mean flashguns do not fire at the critical moment after hours of waiting and all those other problems of composition, focus and exposure.

The development of VHS home video has made badger photography even more exciting because these cameras work to an incredibly low light level and are well worth hiring, if you cannot afford to buy one, for use over a weekend in high summer when the social groups may emerge well before dusk. You can then study your colony in detail at your leisure on your television at home, with freeze-frame for close study of facial and body characteristics, quite apart from the sheer fun of seeing moving pictures of wildlife taken by your very self. I have used 1,000-watt illumination from the house to record feeding badgers on video but it takes a while to get them used to that degree of light.

Look out for stage-struck badgers.

Further ideas & reading

You will be able to find details of your local Badger Group through your local Wildlife Trust (see telephone directory). The National Federation of Badger Groups was formed in January 1986 to co-ordinate the national issues of common concern to Badger Groups. You can become involved in sett surveys, patrols, help in the cases of orphaned or injured badgers and, as you gain in experience, help with the police and the RSPCA in the valuable work of enforcing the laws that relate to the species. Educational and advisory work defuses many potential conflicts between people and badgers. I strongly recommend you join the Mammal Society which brings together everyone, professional or amateur, who is interested in the subject. For further information contact the Society at 15 Cloisters Business Centre, 8 Battersea Park Road, London SW8 4BG.

A very well presented guide for the general reader on the law relating to country sports and the conservation and protection of wildlife is found in :

Parkes, Charlie & Thornley, John, *Fair Game - the law of country sports and the protection of wildlife* (Pelham, London, 1989).

The reference guide to all aspects of the law likely to encountered by rangers and wardens, in easily understood form, also by Charlie Parkes, who is a member of the staff of the Derbyshire Constabulary Training School, includes the law relating to Scotland:

Parkes, Charlie, *Law of the Countryside* (Association of Countryside Rangers, Suffolk, 1983).

The guide for the Police Force Wildlife Liaison Officers I have been able to refer to was produced by the Hertfordshire Constabulary:

Kourik, Steven, Force Wildlife Officer, *Wildlife Law* (Hertfordshire Constabulary, 1991).

For general reading the books on badgers by Ernest Neal are classic works which everyone should read and, although two are out of print, the most recent one covers a vast amount of the material known on the subject. I have also listed the more rare books, which are well worth reading if you can come across them. The books by Chris Ferris such as the extensive extracts from her journals in *The Darkness is Light Enough,* (Michael Joseph, London, 1986) make fascinating reading. The many individual papers published on badgers can be seen in the latest of Dr Neal's books and Dr Kruuk's *The Social Badger,* see below.

Batten, H.M., *The Badger Afield and Underground* (Witherby, London, 1923)

Blakeborough, J.F. and Pease, A.E., *The Life and Habits of the Badger* (Foxhound, London, 1914)

Bradbury, K., 'The badger diet', in Paget, R. J. and Middleton, A.L.V., *Badgers of Yorkshire and Humberside* (Ebor, York, 1974)

Drabble, P., *Badgers at My Window* (Pelham, London, 1969)

Hart-Davis, D., *Eileen Soper's book of Badgers* (Robinson Publishing, London, 1992)

Kruuk, H., *The Social Badger - ecology and behaviour of a group-living carnivore* (Oxford University Press, Oxford, 1989)

Long, C.A. and Killingley, C.A., *The Badgers of the World* (Charles C. Thomas, Springfield, Illinois, 1983)

Neal, E.G., *The Badger* (4th edn), (Collins, London, 1948: 4th edn, 1975)
_____ *Badgers* (Blandford Press, Poole, Dorset, 1977)
_____ *The Natural History of Badgers* (Croom Helm, London, 1986)

Paget, R.J. and Middleton, A.L.V., *Badgers of Yorkshire and Humberside* (Ebor, York, 1974)

Pease, A.E., *The Badger* (Lawrence and Bullen, London, 1898)

Soper, E.A., *When Badgers Wake* (Routledge and Kegan Paul, London, 1955)
_____ *Wild Encounters* (Routledge and Kegan Paul, London, 1957).

Speakman, F.J., *A Forest by Night* (Bell, London, 1965)

If badgers are causing any form of nuisance or are suspected of doing so, you can contact one of several regional ADAS offices for advice and help:

RWSB (Regional Wildlife and
Storage Biologist)
MAFF/ADAS
Block 2, Government Buildings
Lawnswood
Leeds LS16 5PY

RWSB
MAFF/ADAS
Woodthorne
Wolverhampton
WV6 8TQ

RWSB
MAFF/ADAS
Block B, Government Buildings
Brooklands Avenue
Cambridge CB2 2DR

RWSB
MAFF/ADAS
Block A, Government Buildings
Coley Park
Reading

RWSB
MAFF/ADAS
Burghill Road
Westbury-on-Trym
Bristol BS10 6NJ

RWSB
WOAD
Trawsgoed
Aberystwyth
Dyfed SY23 4HT

Index

If you have enjoyed this book, you might be interested to know about other titles in our **British Natural History** series:

BATS
by Phil Richardson
with illustrations by Guy Troughton

DEER
by Norma Chapman
with illustrations by Diana E. Brown

EAGLES
by John A. Love
with illustrations by the author

FROGS AND TOADS
by Trevor Beebee
with illustrations by Guy Troughton

GARDEN CREEPY-CRAWLIES
by Michael Chinery
with illustrations by Guy Troughton

HEDGEHOGS
by Pat Morris
with illustrations by Guy Troughton

OWLS
by Chris Mead
with illustrations by Guy Troughton

RABBITS AND HARES
by Anne McBride
with illustrations by Guy Troughton

ROBINS
by Chris Mead
with illustrations by Kevin Baker

SEALS
by Sheila Anderson
with illustrations by Guy Troughton

SNAKES AND LIZARDS
by Tom Langton
with illustrations by Denys Ovenden

SQUIRRELS
by Jessica Holm
with illustrations by Guy Troughton

STOATS AND WEASELS
by Paddy Sleeman
with illustrations by Guy Troughton

URBAN FOXES
by Stephen Harris
with illustrations by Guy Troughton

WHALES
by Peter Evans
with illustrations by Euan Dunn

WILDCATS
by Mike Tomkies
with illustrations by Denys Ovenden

Each title is priced at £6.95 at time of going to press. If you wish to order a copy or copies, please send a cheque, adding £1 for post and packing, to Whittet Books Ltd, 18 Anley Road, London W14 OBY. For a free catalogue, send s.a.e. to this address.